RIDE

Hudson Valley and Sound Shore

By Dan Goldfischer and Melissa Heffernan
Illustrations by Kathy Murray

Bicycle routes covering Westchester, Rockland and Orange Counties in New York, Greenwich, Conn., and Bergen County, N.J., with some routes extending into Bronx, N.Y., Ridgefield, Conn., and Putnam and Dutchess Counties, N.Y.

WHITE MEADOW PRESS
P.O. BOX 56
BOONTON, N.J. 07005

ACKNOWLEDGEMENTS

We would like to thank the following individuals who contributed ideas, thoughts and encouragement for this book:

Murray and Jean Fischer
Henry Krobetzky
Ronnie Pawelko
Carla Petersen
And particular thanks to Lester Goldfischer for lettering the maps!

Also Available From White Meadow Press:
Bed, Breakfast & Bike/Mid-Atlantic
Bed, Breakfast & Bike/New England
RIDE GUIDE/North Jersey
RIDE GUIDE/Central Jersey
RIDE GUIDE/South Jersey

Please Send For Our Flyer:
White Meadow Press
P.O. Box 56
Boonton, NJ 07005

Library Of Congress Catalog Card Number: 85-52394

ISBN 0-933855-01-X
Bed, Breakfast & Bike™ and RIDE GUIDE™ are trademarks of White Meadow Press.

CONTENTS

INTRODUCTION

North of New York City lies a river valley of incredible beauty and rich history. The Hudson Valley is not a major tourist mecca, but that's only because the city at its mouth draws the majority of visitors. The scenic splendors and interesting craft and antique shops, museums and restored mansions in the Hudson Valley require a slow pace for proper touring. Thus, the area is an ideal place for bicycle touring.

Westchester County residents are lucky enough to have two bodies of water at their doorstep—the Hudson and Long Island Sound. The scenery along the Sound may not be as dramatic as the Hudson Highlands, but is beautiful in its own way with water vistas, sea bird life, and large homes and tidy villages near the shore.

The great thing about cycling in the Hudson Valley or along the Sound is that you don't have to drive for hours to reach the starting point of your ride. All the rides in this guide start at places no more than 90 minutes from New York City by car or train. Yet when you are cycling along a rural road in Northern Westchester with nothing but woods and deer in any direction; you could easily picture yourself in northern Maine.

A day with your bicycle should be an enjoyable experience. For thousands of bike club members, those weekend pedals are the highlights of their week. If you are not accustomed to cycling 20-50 miles in a day, you might consider joining your local club. Members are always eager to give newcomers tips and encouragement.

Two keys to getting the most pleasure out of the cycling part of your outing are good equipment and a good attitude toward hills. Having a multispeed bike that's working well with fully inflated tires makes a big difference. And seeing hills as challenges rather than punishment will make you feel that much better when you crest the summit.

Our guide is not designed for "professional" cyclists whose seats rarely leave the saddle. The routes feature the points of interest, well-known and little-known, that make the Hudson Valley and Sound Shore such interesting areas to tour. So plan an early start, bring your camera and swimsuit and stop often along the way. That way, you will not simply go for a bike ride, but rather a bike tour, the most fun, most leisurely and healthiest way to tour!

Read the next section on How To Use This Book, then pack RIDE GUIDE in your bike bag, and happy cycling!

HOW TO USE THIS BOOK

Ride Guide/Hudson Valley and Sound Shore is organized by sections according to route starting points. Thus, Central Westchester includes rides heading into Northern Westchester, and the Bergen and Rockland Section includes two rides that go into Orange County. The name of each route generally consists of the point of origin and the destination. All routes return to their starting points. Directions are often given for combining routes to make larger tours. Read the section introductions for summaries of routes within each section.

Getting closer to deciding where to ride? If you are an experienced touring cyclist, points of interest will probably be the deciding factor. Novice and intermediate riders should closely examine the following factors, all listed in the beginning of each route description:

Mileage: If you've never ridden more than 20 miles a day, it might not be a good idea to jump into a 50-mile ride, but you should be able to handle 25 or 30 miles. If you've overestimated your ability, the map will offer short-cuts back to the starting point.

Terrain: Far more important than mileage! The Hudson Valley and interior Westchester are hilly to various degrees, and we tell you whether a route is gently rolling or "memorably challenging." Decide what you can handle, then challenge yourself a little! It is no disgrace to walk your bike when you're tired.

Traffic: As well as being a hilly area, this is a populated area, especially closer to New York City. Cars are a big factor in your riding enjoyment (especially on the skinny, shoulderless roads that are popular here). While every effort is made to stick to quiet back roads, sometimes short distances on busy thoroughfares are unavoidable, and we will mention that in this category of the route description.

Road Conditions: If you have regular clincher tires, you shouldn't have to worry about poorly paved roads or dirt roads. We do not shy away from these roads because they often have the nicest scenery. So we mention in this category how good the overall road conditions are, and whether there is any dirt or poor pavement.

Now you've picked your ride and are ready to go. **Directions to Starting Point** tell you how to get there by car. **Metro-North Directions** (for rides east of the Hudson and from Bear Mountain) provide train directions from Grand Central Terminal in New York or the suburbs. To obtain the permit necessary for bringing your bike on the train, send $5 to Metro-North Commuter Railroad, 347 Madison Ave., New York, NY 10017. Note that bikes are not allowed on rush hour trains.

Along with RIDE GUIDE, it is a good idea to bring a local or regional roadmap if you are going to an area for the first time. This will allow you to depart from the route for your own exploration, and will help you if residential developments or road work alter the street pattern (a frequent occurrence in this growing region). Also, turning around or swiping street signs are still popular ''pranks'' and are the most frequent causes of missed turns.

The maps should be used for general orientation: they are not drawn to scale. Use the cue sheet to determine the next street or landmark.

How to Use the Cue Sheets:

The two columns of mileage figures are **point to point** (left column), which represents the distance from the previous turn, and **cumulative** (right column), which represents the distance from the starting point.

Abbreviations in the **turns** column are:

L	Left
R	Right
S	Straight
BR	Bear Right
BL	Bear Left
SL	Sharp Left
SR	Sharp Right

In the **streets/landmarks** column, only the street you are going on is printed in **boldface.** Intersecting roads are printed in lightface. *Italics* are used to indicate directions to connecting routes.

A (T) is an intersection where the road you are on ends at another road. You must go right or left; you cannot go straight.

RIDE GUIDE
ROUTE STARTING POINTS

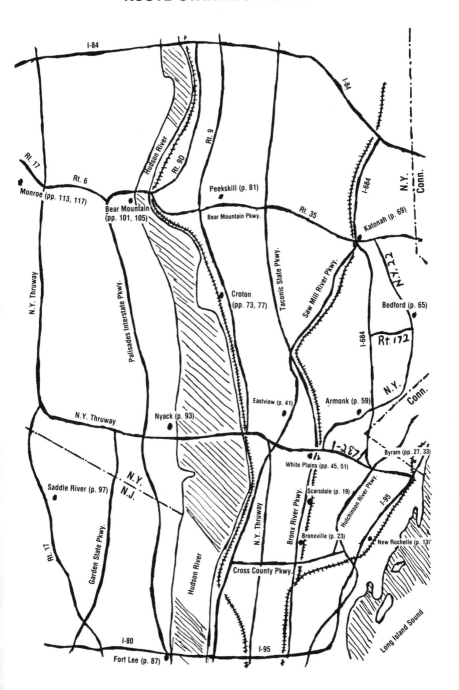

RIDES STARTING IN

SOUTHERN WESTCHESTER AND GREENWICH

Old-time New York City residents still think of anything north of Fordham Road in the Bronx as "the country" or "upstate." Inhabitants of more northerly locales such as Yorktown or North Salem picture downtown Mt. Vernon and Yonkers when they think of Southern Westchester and equate the entire section with New York City. The reality is somewhere in between: while Southern Westchester has its busy cities and crowded thoroughfares, there is still plenty of pleasant, almost country-like cycling to be had in this section, particularly in the wealthier towns.

Cycling in Southern Westchester means quiet suburban streets with large homes of every architectural style: New York City's corporate executives have been commuting from Westchester for over a century and it is only recently that look-alike homes have become more numerous than distinctive domiciles. Rye, Scarsdale, Pelham and Greenwich in particular have some real palaces.

This section features Long Island Sound, a salt water body known as the "Times Square" of recreational boating. On a good summer weekend you can have difficulty seeing the water for all the sailboats on the Sound. Nature lovers appreciate the marshland and saltwater bird life of the Sound Shore area.

For the cyclist, Southern Westchester and Greenwich means flat and fairly easy going near the Sound, and a bit hillier inland, particularly in Greenwich. **Sound Shore Wanderer** goes south from New Rochelle and heads down to the very bottom of the Sound at Throgs Neck, with its impressive view of Manhattan. The return includes City Island, a seafood lovers' paradise, and numerous water views and beaches all the way up to Larchmont.

Scarsdale-Playland starts inland and reaches the water at Mamaroneck. Stops en route to Playland include a fantastic nature preserve where woods meet water and egrets nest in marshes. And anyone who grew up in Westchester knows the magic of Playland, the art-deco masterpiece of amusement parks.

Westchester's county government has been encouraging cycling since the mid-'70s by closing off the Bronx River Parkway for four hours each Sunday from April through October (except holiday weekends). Autos are banished from Tuckahoe to White Plains from 10 AM to 2 PM Sundays, and cyclists can enjoy the lush greenery of America's first landscaped parkway. For riders who want to enjoy this serene strip located in a very densely populated corridor but don't want to wait until Sunday, **Bronx River Valley** presents parallel routes to the parkway on quiet residential streets and recently completed bike paths.

Greenwich is one of the wealthiest towns in the U.S. It is also a cyclist's paradise with its varied and interesting terrain ranging from Sound flat to New England inland hilly. The roads are quiet and well-paved, with occasional country stores for fuel along the way. **Greenwich Sampler** includes a little inland hilly and a little Sound (relatively) flat. **Greenwich-Armonk** is more challenging in terms of terrain, and gets farther out into the remote "back country" of large estates and horse farms. The latter route includes stops at a cartoon museum, the outdoor sculpture garden at Pepsico headquarters, the state university at Purchase, N.Y., and Westchester County Airport.

Southern Westchester and Greenwich have something for every cyclist to enjoy. City slickers can find country riding close by (in Greenwich), while riders used to farms and woods may wish to gaze at large homes by Long Island Sound. Enjoy!

SOUND SHORE WANDERER 34.2 miles

Terrain: Mostly flat, since this ride follows the shore of Long Island Sound.

Traffic: Urban traffic can be expected in New Rochelle, moderate elsewhere. There is surprisingly little traffic in the Bronx section of the route.

Road Conditions: Fair to good, except for the residential section south of Pelham Bay Park, which is undergoing extensive construction.

Points of Interest: Large homes in Pelham and Larchmont; **Bartow-Pell Mansion** (restored historic home); **view of New York City** from Throgs Neck; **City Island** (seafood restaurants and shops); Sound Shore parks: **Orchard Beach, Glen Island, Hudson Park** and **Manor Park.**

The Sound Shore does not play an important part in American history, as the Hudson Valley does, but it is definitely worth exploration if only for the spectacular water views and the salt air.

This route covers a populous area and some parts of the ride go over busy streets, so riders should brush up on their defensive cycling skills. But mingled with the unavoidable suburban thoroughfares are quiet suburban roads with huge homes, a New England fishing village located within the borders of New York City, and fine waterside parks.

Start in New Rochelle, "The Queen City of the Sound." Pass the College of New Rochelle, the oldest Catholic women's college in New York State. Ride by some huge mansions in Pelham before heading south into the Bronx.

Your goal is to reach SUNY Maritime, directly under the Throgs Neck Bridge, with its impressive views of bridges, the New York skyline and planes approaching LaGuardia Airport. Enroute you will ride through Pelham Bay Park and down quiet, clean and safe residential streets that belie the traditional image of the Bronx.

The return from Throgs Neck takes you to City Island, a unique collection of boats, restaurants and antique shops. The entire island is only two blocks wide!

Then it's more Sound Shore wandering in Westchester—to two beautiful parks in New Rochelle (Glen Island and Hudson Park) and one in Larchmont (Manor Park). Note that these are county or municipal parks and during the summer technically require a residence pass, but generally cyclists are not checked. Swimming is available at Orchard Beach in the Bronx as well as at Glen Island and Hudson Park.

SOUND SHORE WANDERER (continued)

Directions to Starting Point: The route starts at **Clinton Place and South Division Street in New Rochelle.** Take Exit 15 off I-95 and follow U.S. 1 north about a mile into the business district of New Rochelle, then turn right onto Division Street. Municipal parking is available on both sides of Division St. one block south of Main Street (U.S. 1).

Metro-North Directions: Take a New Haven Line Stamford local to New Rochelle. Carry your bike up the stairs on the middle of the platform, and exit onto the street (do not cross the tracks). Ride to the right two blocks to Division Street, then left three blocks to the corner of Clinton Place, the start of the ride.

POINT TO POINT	CUME	TURN	STREET/LANDMARK
0.0	0.0		Start at intersection of **Clinton Place** and **South Division Street** in New Rochelle. Proceed south on **South Division Street** (away from Main St.)
0.1	0.1	R	**Prospect St.**
0.0	0.1	L	**Centre Ave.** (T)
0.3	0.4	R	**Elm St.** (traffic light). **College of New Rochelle** will be on the left shortly after the turn
0.6	1.0	L	**Weyman Ave.** (T)
0.2	1.2	R	**Mt. Tom Rd.**
0.6	1.8	L	**Rockledge Dr.** (stop sign)
0.2	2.0	R	**Hillcrest Dr.** (T)
0.4	2.4	L	**Pelhamdale Ave.** (T)
0.3	2.7	R	**Shore Rd.** (T)
1.2	3.9		**Bartow-Pell Mansion** on left
0.4	4.3	S	Go halfway around the traffic circle toward **City Island-Shore Road South**
0.9	5.2	L	Carefully cross road near landfill (on left) and ride onto the service road (near landfill), against traffic
0.2	5.4	L	Enter bike path in **Pelham Bay Park.** Head south on the paths toward **Rice Stadium**
0.9	6.3	L	**Middletown Rd.** after exiting bike path in front of Rice Stadium
0.1	6.4	R	**Stadium Ave.**
0.8	7.2	BR	At fork onto **Dean Ave.** (Prospect Rest Nursing Home on left)
0.4	7.6	R	**Philip Ave.** (curve right)
0.0	7.6	L	**Clarence Ave.**
0.4	8.0	R	**Schley Ave.** (curve right)

continued

SOUND SHORE WANDERER (continued)

POINT TO POINT	CUME	TURN	STREET/LANDMARK
0.1	8.1	L	**Throgs Neck Expwy. (service road)** (stop sign)
0.6	8.7	R	**Prentiss Ave.** (stop sign). Cross highway
0.3	9.0	BL	At traffic light onto **Pennyfield Ave.** (toward SUNY Maritime College)
0.6	9.6		**SUNY Maritime College on left.** Sign in at guardhouse to ride through college (views of Manhattan, water and bridges). Return the way you came on **Pennyfield Ave.**
0.9	10.5	BR	At traffic light to cross over highway
0.0	10.5	L	**Throgs Neck Expwy. (service road)**
0.7	11.2	L	At stop and T to continue on **Throgs Neck Expwy. (service road)**
0.6	11.8	S	At stop sign onto **Fairfax Ave.**; continue to parallel highway
0.3	12.1	L	**Waterbury Ave.** (T)
0.1	12.2	R	**Kearney Ave.** (T). After turn go straight on **service road (Bruckner Blvd.)** which parallels highway (Kearney Ave. bears right)
0.5	12.7	BL	To continue on service road (Pelham Bay Park is on the right)
0.5	13.2	BR	Toward **Orchard Beach and City Island**
1.0	14.2	R	At traffic light (toward **City Island**) after passing draw bridge
0.7	14.9	S	Go halfway around traffic circle toward **City Island**
0.7	15.6	BR	After going over bridge onto **City Island Ave.**
1.3	16.9		**U-turn** at end of **City Island Ave.**
0.9	17.8	R	**Ditmars St.**
0.1	17.9	L	**Minnieford Ave.**
0.5	18.4	L	**Bridge St.** (street sign on right hidden under tree branch)
0.1	18.5	R	Cross bridge
0.6	19.1	R	At traffic circle toward **Orchard Beach**
0.8	19.9		**U-turn** at Orchard Beach
0.7	20.6	R	Toward **Hutchinson River Pkwy.**
0.3	20.9	R	At traffic circle onto **Shore Rd. North**
2.3	23.2	R	At traffic light toward **Glen Island**
0.2	23.4	S	Cross bridge onto **Glen Island**
0.5	23.9		Circle island and return over the draw bridge
0.5	24.4	R	**Harbor Lane**
0.1	24.5	L	**Ft. Slocum Rd.** (T) (no sign)

continued

SOUND SHORE WANDERER (continued)

POINT TO POINT	CUME	TURN	STREET/LANDMARK
0.2	24.7	R	**Pelham Rd.** (T) (no sign)
1.1	25.8	BR	**Hudson Park Rd.**
0.4	26.2		**U turn** at the end of the road in **Hudson Park**
0.5	26.7	SR	**Pelham Rd.** (traffic light)
0.2	26.9	L	**Echo Ave.** (curve left)
0.2	27.1	R	**Main St.**
0.8	27.9	R	**Emerson Ave.** (by Shell station)
0.1	28.0	L	**Chester Place**
0.2	28.2	R	**Dillon Rd.** (T)
0.1	28.3	S	Road changes names to **Pryer Manor Rd.**
0.6	28.9	L	**Pryer Lane** (T)
0.0	28.9	R	**Helena Ave.**
0.3	29.2	R	**Beach Ave.** (stop sign)
0.1	29.3	R	**Park Ave.** (stop sign)
0.1	29.4	BR	At fork (no sign) onto **Circle Dr.**
0.2	29.6		Entrance to **Manor Park** on left. Use bike rack. Continue on **Circle Dr.** after visiting park
0.2	29.8	L	At fork and stop onto **Park Ave.**
0.1	29.9	R	**Prospect Ave.** (unusual house one block up on right)
0.1	30.0	R	**Maple Ave.**
0.2	30.2	L	**Circle Ave.** (T)
0.0	30.2	R	**Woodbine Ave.** (stop sign)
0.1	30.3	L	**Larchmont Ave.** (stop sign)
0.9	31.2	L	**Palmer Ave.** (by Baskin Robbins)
1.5	32.7	BR	At fork. Follow signs toward **Rt. 95**
0.2	32.9	BL	At fork after going under highway. Follow signs for **North Rt. 95/Division St.**
0.1	33.0	BR	At fork. Follow "hospital" signs
0.3	33.3		At traffic circle, go two-thirds the way around toward Rt. 1. You will be on **Memorial Highway,** which becomes **Division St.**
0.9	34.2		Intersection of **Clinton and South Division Streets** (end of route)

SOUND SHORE WANDERER
(34.2 miles)

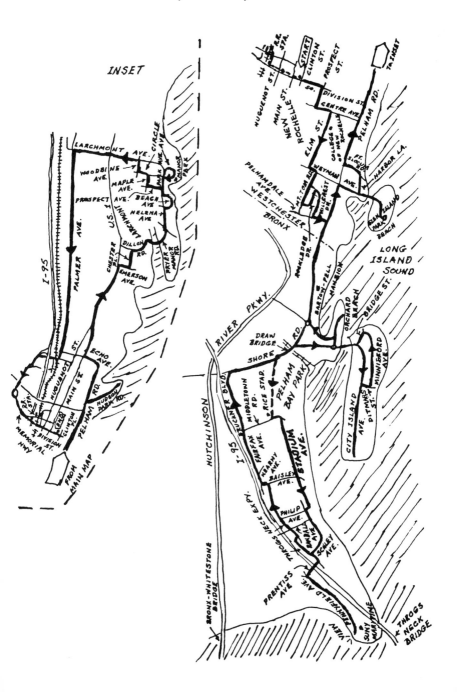

SCARSDALE-PLAYLAND
(29.5 miles)

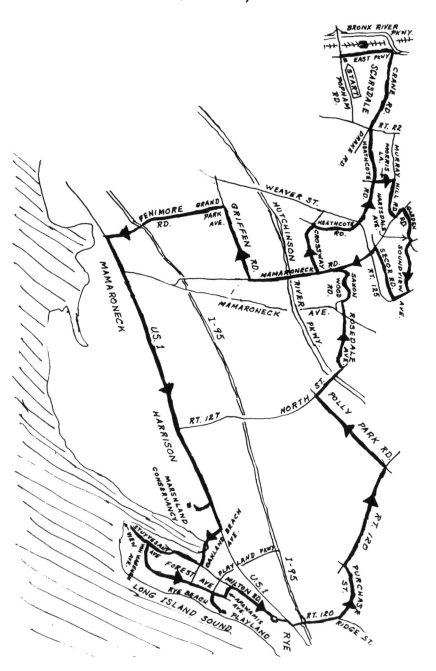

SCARSDALE-PLAYLAND   29.5 miles

Terrain: Gently rolling. Some longer climbs out of the Bronx River Valley and heading inland from the Sound.
Traffic: Mostly quiet suburban streets, with some short stretches on busier roads.
Road Conditions: Very good, except bumpy Griffen Rd.
Points of Interest: Large homes; Harbor views in Mamaroneck and Rye; **Marshlands Conservancy** (hiking and nature exhibit); **Rye Beach; Playland Amusement Park; Square House** (Rye Historical Society).

Southern **Westchester,** while being for the most part an urban, built-up section of suburban New York, does have its quieter parts. The wealthy towns of Scarsdale, Mamaroneck, Rye, and Harrison have broad, smooth roads with large estates, sections of undeveloped woods and even a horse farm or two.

Playland, destination of this route, is the finest example of an art-deco amusement park in the U.S. Located on the Sound, the flower-lined midway capped by the tall music tower is etched into many a Westchesterite's memory. The county-run attraction is still a fun and free place to visit, and cycling there beats the cost and hassle of parking. Try out the legendary Dragon Coaster for some thrilling terrain.

On the way to Playland, be sure to stop at Marshlands Convervancy. The nature preserve has a beautiful trail leading through woods to wetlands by the Sound, where waterbirds such as egrets and great blue herons can be observed.

Rye Beach is an excellent swimming beach, but is generally reserved for town residents and their guests. Swimming is available at Playland.

Directions to Starting Point: This route begins at the intersection of **East Parkway and Popham Rd.** in downtown Scarsdale. Take the Bronx River Pkwy. to Exit 12 and proceed along East Parkway to the traffic light, which is Popham Rd. Metered parking is available on village streets; longer-term parking can be found in a garage across the railroad tracks and south of the train station.
Metro-North Directions: Take a Harlem Line White Plains North local to Scarsdale. Carry your bike up the rear stairs on the platform, which lead to Popham Rd. (the street which crosses over the tracks). East Parkway is to your left, paralleling the railroad.
Note: This route may be combined with the Bronx River Valley ride (p. 23) to make a 57-mile route. On Bicycle Sundays (see section introduction), you cannot drive on the Bronx River Pkwy. We suggest you park your car in Bronxville and ride up the Parkway to Scarsdale to begin the route. This will add 8 miles to the round-trip distance.

SCARSDALE-PLAYLAND (continued)

POINT TO POINT	CUME	TURN	STREET/LANDMARK
0.0	0.0	L	Start at the intersection of **East Parkway** and **Popham Rd.** With your back to the railroad, turn **left** on **East Parkway**
0.2	0.2	R	**Crane Rd.**
0.6	0.8	BL	**Heathcote Rd.** (Cross Rt. 22)
0.8	1.6	L	**Morris Lane** (traffic light)
0.6	2.2	R	**Murray Hill Rd.** (T)
0.4	2.6	L	**Mamaroneck Rd.** (traffic light)
0.4	3.0	R	**Garden Rd.**
0.5	3.5	S	At stop sign. Road changes name to **Hartsdale Ave.** at White Plains city line
0.2	3.7	R	**Soundview Ave.** (traffic light)
0.6	4.3	R	**Old Mamaroneck Rd./Rt. 125** (traffic light)
0.8	5.1	R	**Secor Rd.**
0.3	5.4	L	**Mamaroneck Rd.** (traffic light)
0.6	6.0	BL	At fork to continue on **Mamaroneck Rd.** (Crossway goes right)
0.9	6.9	R	**Griffen Rd.** (at end of stone wall)
1.1	8.0	L	**Grand Park Ave.** (which shortly becomes **Fenimore Rd.**)
2.2	10.2	L	**Boston Post Rd./Rt. 1** (T)
1.3	11.5		Farm stand on right
0.7	12.2	R	Driveway into **Marshlands Conservancy**
0.2	12.4		Start of hiking trail to Long Island Sound. After hiking, cycle back the way you came in (water and restrooms available here)
0.2	12.6	R	**Rt. 1** (T)
0.6	13.2	R	**Oakland Beach Ave.** (traffic light)
0.6	13.8	R	**Milton Rd.** (traffic light) (**store** on right shortly after turn)
0.5	14.3	L	**Stuyvesant Ave.** (blinking light)
1.1	15.4		**U-turn** by entrance to American Yacht Club (end of public road). Enjoy the view of Milton Harbor!
0.5	15.9	R	**Van Wagenen Ave.**
0.2	16.1	L	**Forest Ave.** (curve left)
0.9	17.0		Entrance to **Rye Beach** on right
0.4	17.4	R	**Playland Pkwy.** (traffic light)
0.3	17.7		**Playland** entrance. Return the way you came in
0.4	18.1	R	**Forest Ave.** (traffic light)
0.3	18.4	L	**Apawamis Ave.** (traffic light)
0.4	18.8	R	**Milton Rd.** (T)
0.6	19.4	L	At traffic circle to continue on **Milton Rd.**

continued

SCARSDALE-PLAYLAND (continued)

POINT TO POINT	CUME	TURN	STREET/LANDMARK
0.1	19.5	S	At traffic light, onto **Rt. 1 North**
0.0	19.5	BL	At fork (immediately after last turn) onto **Rt. 120/ Purchase St.**
			Note: Bicycles are officially banned from this section of Purchase St. due to the danger of cars backing out of diagonal parking spaces. An alternate is to turn **sharp left** at this corner onto narrow **Haviland Lane** (marked with a "Do Not Enter" sign) and carefully ride against traffic behind the stores. Turn right at the street by the railroad tracks, then left onto Purchase St. to resume the route. The **Square House** of the Rye Historical Society is on the right at the Haviland Lane turn.
0.8	20.3	S	At red blinking light to continue on **Purchase St.** (Ridge St. goes right)
0.5	20.8	R	At red blinking light to continue on **Rt. 120**
0.6	21.4	L	**Polly Park Rd.** (traffic light)
1.6	23.0	R	**North St./Rt. 127**(traffic light)
0.4	23.4	L	**Rosedale Ave.**
1.2	24.6	S	Cross Mamaroneck Ave.
0.2	24.8	R	**Saxon Wood Rd.** (T)
1.3	26.1	L	**Mamaroneck Rd.** (T)
0.2	26.3	BR	At fork onto **Crossway**
0.5	26.8	R	**Heathcote Rd.**
0.5	27.3	S	Cross Palmer Ave.
1.4	28.7	BR	**Crane Rd.** (Cross Rt. 22)
0.6	29.3	L	**East Parkway**
0.2	29.5		Intersection of **East Parkway** and **Popham Rd.** (end of route)

BRONX RIVER VALLEY
(24.0 miles)

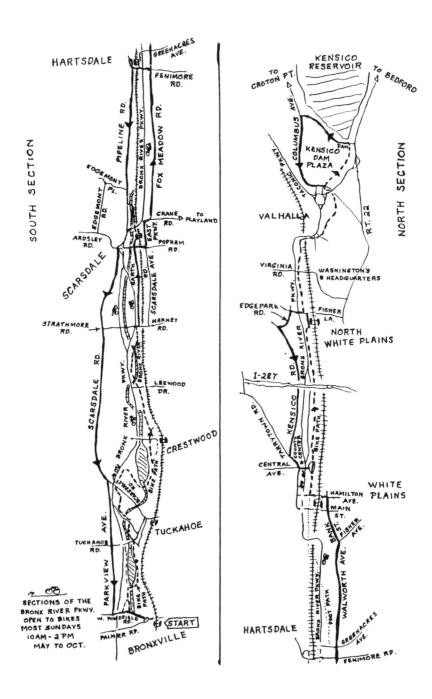

BRONX RIVER VALLEY   24.0 miles

As noted in the introduction to this section, Westchester County closes seven miles of the Bronx River Pkwy. to auto traffic for several hours each Sunday. What about cyclists who wish to ride in this pretty area when only autos may use the parkway? This route presents parallel roads and bike paths that follow the Bronx River Valley. It is described in narrative format rather than a cue sheet because there are so many turns in such a short distance.

Start at the **Bronxville station** and pedal west on **Pondfield Rd.** Signs on the traffic circle on the toward-New York-side of the station will identify the correct road. Shortly before Pondfield Rd. crosses the parkway, turn right on either of two **bike path** spurs. After a short, steep rise and fall, both spurs join to form one path, then separate again at the bottom of a duck pond. Choose the path on the **right side of the pond** (crossing a footbridge immediately). This will enable you to avoid carrying your bike up stairs at Tuckahoe Rd. The pond and lawns are popular in season with local fowl-feeders and sunbathers.

The path crosses **Tuckahoe Rd.** as the road forks to enter Tuckahoe. Look closely for fast-moving traffic as you cross this street. Next the path runs on a striped-off area of the **Elm St. on-ramp** to the parkway before continuing on its own separate right of way.

At **Scarsdale Rd.** you have reached the lower end of the Bronx River Pkwy. closing area, and if you happen to be here between 10 and 2 on a bicycle Sunday, take to the highway. If not, continue on the path, which crosses a couple of residential streets before appearing to backtrack in order to cross a stream at the bottom of another duck pond. You will ride alongside this pond for a ways. Take the left fork to stay closer to the river as you approach the **Crestwood railroad station.**

After crossing the entrance road to the station parking lot, the path follows a driveway leading to a parkway maintenance garage, then returns to its own right of way. The next two miles to the end of the path at Harney Rd. has only one road crossing, and bridges the Bronx River several times.

BRONX RIVER VALLEY (continued)

Carefully cross **Harney Rd.** at path's end onto **Garth Rd.** (do not cross the parkway or railroad). This street features fine old tudor apartment houses. At the traffic light (**Popham Rd.**), turn **right**, cross the railroad and turn **left** onto **East Parkway.** You may wish to walk your turn here, as this is a congested area.

Follow East Parkway through downtown Scarsdale, which resembles a suburb of London more than a suburb of New York. Curve **right** onto **Crane Rd.** at the parkway entrance, then take the first **left** onto **Fox Meadow Rd.** This is a flat, wide, quiet street flanked with large homes. Continue about 4 miles straight into White Plains—the road will change names twice, first to **Walworth Ave.,** then to **Fisher Ave.**

Turn **left** onto **Bank St.,** then **left** again onto **Hamilton Ave.** You will find a **bike path** between the railroad and the parkway: follow the path past the **County Center** parking lot all the way to the foot of Kensico Dam. The only turn on the path is at the **North White Plains** railroad station: Do not go under the tracks, but rather turn **left,** ride through the **station parking lot,** then make a **left** on **Fisher Lane.** The path resumes as a **right** turn just past a steel-deck bridge. You may wish to visit **Washington's Headquarters.** To do so, turn **right** where **Virginia Rd.** crosses the path.

By the time you reach **Kensico Dam,** you will be warmed up for the only serious hill of this route—a climb up an old brick auto road to the top of the dam. Cross the busy road at the entrance to the park below the dam, make a slight right turn and proceed up this tree-lined, smooth **brick path.** At the top, turn **left.** Admire the view of Kensico Reservoir on your right and central Westchester on your left as you cross the dam. A good **hot dog stand** with a picnic table is on your left as you round the bend after the dam. It is situated well back from the road.

Follow the road alongside the reservoir for a mile or so until you reach a T by some large waterworks buildings. Turn **left** onto **Columbus Ave.,** and enjoy a speedy descent into Valhalla. Watch your speed! The hill gets steep before you know it.

BRONX RIVER VALLEY (continued)

Turn **right** onto the **bike path** and ride back to White Plains. For those who wish a somewhat smoother ride, at the steel deck bridge (**Fisher Lane**), turn **right**, cross the parkway, make the first **left** on **Edgepark Rd.**, and then **left** at the T onto **Kensico Rd.**, which takes you to the back of the County Center building. Here you must cross the parkway to rejoin the bike path. Note that getting to Kensico Rd. involves a steep climb.

In White Plains, you may wish to return the way you came (**left** onto **Main St., right** onto **Bank St., right** at **Fisher Ave.**) or attempt to follow the bike path. We say "attempt" because the path degenerates into a footpath quickly, and a poorly maintained one at that. But for cyclists with a sense of adventure, the path will let you out by the Hartsdale station. Just be prepared to walk muddy or thin sections and watch out for one parkway underpass with head clearance so low you will *have* to walk.

If you are on **Fisher Ave.**, which becomes **Walworth Ave.**, turn **right** at the second Hartsdale traffic light onto **Fenimore Rd.** Cross the tracks by the **Hartsdale station,** then turn right into the **station plaza.** You will notice a small road going under the overpass you were just on and paralleling the railroad: this is **Pipeline Rd.**, a straight, flat shot to Scarsdale with nothing but woods on one side and the tracks on the other. About one-quarter mile after you pass the one side street (Edgemont Pl.), look for a **small opening in the guardrail** on your left. Walk your bike down a path and over a **footbridge** crossing the skinny Bronx River. Turn right on the **path** next to the tracks, which leads you directly into the **Scarsdale station** parking lot.

At the end of the station road, turn **right** at the light onto **Popham Rd.** Cross the parkway, then turn **left** onto **Scarsdale Rd.,** which forks off the southbound parkway entrance ramp. Follow Scarsdale Rd. to **Strathmore Rd.** At this point, you may either turn **left,** cross the parkway and return on the **path** from **Harney Rd.** to **Pondfield Rd.,** or go **straight** on **Scarsdale Rd.** for several miles to **Parkview Ave.** Turn **right** on Parkview to **Pondfield Rd.,** then turn **left** to return to **Bronxville station.**

BRONX RIVER VALLEY (continued)

Directions To Starting Point: Bronxville station is located off the Bronx River Pkwy. Take the Pondfield Rd. exit from the northbound parkway and turn right. From the southbound parkway, turn right on Scarsdale Rd., left on Parkview Ave., then left on Pondfield Rd.

Metro-North Directions: Take a Harlem Division local bound for North White Plains to the Bronxville station.

Note: Three other rides in this guide start at places along this route: Scarsdale-Playland (p. 19), White Plains-Croton Point (p. 45) and White Plains-Bedford (p. 51).

GREENWICH SAMPLER   26.1 miles

Terrain: Rolling, with several "shorties but steepies" (hills, that is). Very gentle terrain near the Sound (last 11 miles of route).
Traffic: Incredibly light, considering how close you are to the metropolis. A few short busy stretches, noted on the cue sheet.
Road Conditions: Superb. Greenwich has a low per-capita pothole rate.
Points of Interest: The amazing contrasts of the town of **Greenwich**—from the wealthy, woodsy **backcountry** to the New England charm of the **shoreside villages; Binney Park; The Bruce Museum; Greenwich Point** and **Byram Parks.**

It is possible to ride a good distance entirely within the boundaries of the town of Greenwich and see a sampling of the entire New England region—from the woodsy, hilly interior with its stone walls, ponds and streams, to neat villages and saltwater vistas.

Start in Byram, a section of Greenwich that used to call itself East Port Chester after its busy neighbor across the Byram River. Head up pretty Pemberwick Rd. to the bustling inland settlement of Glenville. Before reaching Glenville, you might wish to look at an old mill that has been converted to shops, offices and restaurants. A particularly impressive waterfall, where the Byram River goes over the mill dam, is visible from the back of the complex.

The ride from west to east over colorfully named streets such as Clapboard Ridge, Dingletown Road and Cat Rock Road takes you over numerous ridges which will alternately give your low gears and brakes good workouts. Look for several very old graveyards along the way that tell of the time this was a thriving farming section.

Cross the Mianus River, then head down to Old Greenwich. This is probably the neatest of the New Englandy villages within Greenwich. Binney Park is so picture perfect that many wedding parties are photographed by the pond here, and it is a good lunch spot.

The route back heads out toward Greenwich Point, where excellent views of bay and sound are visible from the road. Unfortunately, Greenwich Point Park, which is the nicest park on the Sound, is open only to town residents. From November to March the gatehouse is empty, and during slow non-summer weekdays cyclists might be able to ask nicely to enter for a ride around. It is worth the trouble, because there are several miles of roads in the park with superb views, especially on clear days when New York is visible.

Next head through Riverside, a section of wealthy homes. After crossing the railroad on an ornate old iron bridge, look for what has to be the smallest general store in the region on your left. There is no sign out front, but the crowd of local kids with their banana-seat bikes leaning on the fence is a dead giveaway that the small white house behind the fence is a store.

GREENWICH SAMPLER (continued)

Cyclists who enjoy modern art may wish to stop at the Bruce Museum, an excellent small art and science museum. Return to Byram on a road that changes names three times in a little over a mile. Take a last look at the Sound in Byram Park before returning to your car or train. If you are hungry for pizza or pasta after the ride, Byram sports several excellent Italian restaurants.

Directions to Starting Point: Mead Ave. and Mill St. in the Byram section of Greenwich is located close to Exit 2 of I-95 (the Connecticut Turnpike). Turn left onto Delavan Ave. if exiting off northbound I-95 and right if coming off southbound I-95. In several blocks you will see a firehouse on the left. Mead Ave. is the left turn just past the firehouse, and Delavan Ave. changes its name to Mill St. at this point. Park on the street or in nearby municipal lots.

Metro-North Directions: Take a New Haven Line Stamford local to Port Chester. Carry your bike down the stairs at the front of the platform, then ride away from the tracks on Highland St. Cross Main St. (Rt. 1), then take the next left (Abendroth Ave.). At the T, turn right onto Mill St. Cross the little bridge into Connecticut, then turn left at the traffic light onto North Water St. This is the intersection at Mile 0.1 of the cue sheet.

GREENWICH SAMPLER (continued)

POINT TO POINT	CUME	TURN	STREET/LANDMARK
0.0	0.0	L	Start at the corner of **Mead Ave.** and **Mill St.** While standing at the end of Mead Ave., ride **left** onto **Mill St.**
0.1	0.1	R	**N. Water St.** (traffic light)
0.5	0.6	L	**Byram Rd.** (T)
0.2	0.8	R	**W. Putnam Ave./Rt. 1** (T)
0.0	0.8	L	Get in the left turn lane immediately and turn into **Pemberwick Rd.**
1.9	2.7		Old mill and falls on left
0.1	2.8	L	**Glenville Rd.** (T)
0.1	2.9	R	**Riversville Rd.** (traffic light)
0.5	3.4	R	**Pecksland Rd.**
1.5	4.9	L	**Round Hill Rd.** (T)
0.7	5.6	R	**Clapboard Ridge Rd.**
0.9	6.5	R	**Lake Ave.** (T)
0.0	6.5	L	Immediate **left** to continue on **Clapboard Ridge Rd.**
1.1	7.6	L	At T and stop sign to continue on **Clapboard Ridge Rd.** (Grahamton Lane goes left)
0.3	7.9	L	**North St.** (T)
0.2	8.1	R	**Dingletown Rd.**
1.3	9.4	R	**Stanwich Rd.** (T)
0.1	9.5	L	Immediate **left** onto **Cat Rock Rd.**
1.9	11.4	L	**Valley Rd.** (T)
0.2	11.6	R	**Palmer Hill Rd.**
0.1	11.7	R	**Sheephill Rd.** (first right after bridge over Mianus River)
0.7	12.4	L	**Sound Beach Ave. Extension**
0.5	12.9	S	Cross E. Putnam Ave./Rt. 1
0.5	13.4	BR	At little rotary to continue on **Sound Beach Ave.** Laddins Rock Rd. goes left. **Binney Park** will be on your right after turning
1.3	14.7	R	**Shore Rd.** (T)
0.8	15.5		Entrance to Greenwich Point Park. Cycle back the way you came
0.8	16.3	L	**Sound Beach Ave.**
0.9	17.2	L	**West End Ave.** (traffic light)
0.3	17.5	L	At little rotary onto **Riverside Ave.**

continued

GREENWICH SAMPLER (continued)

POINT TO POINT	CUME	TURN	STREET/LANDMARK
0.8	18.3	**BR**	At fork to continue on **Riverside Ave.** Indian Head Rd. goes left (no sign)
0.5	18.8	**L**	At stop sign to continue on **Riverside Ave.** Cross old iron overpass over railroad tracks. (Oval Ave. goes right)
0.1	18.9		Store disguised as small white house on your left shortly after crossing the tracks
0.5	19.4	**L**	**Rt. 1** (traffic light). CAUTION: Busy road
0.3	19.7	**L**	**River Rd.** (next traffic light. CAUTION: Do a "two-point turn" from the right side of the road)
0.7	20.4	**L**	**Strickland Ave.** (Cos Cob Historical Society directly in front of you at this turn. Turn **right** at this corner if you wish to view more old Cos Cob homes)
0.3	20.7	**L**	**Sound Shore Dr.** (Street goes under railroad immediately)
0.4	21.1	**L**	**Indian Field Rd.** (traffic light). Cross over I-95 after turn
0.3	21.4	**R**	**Bruce Park Dr.**
0.5	21.9	**R**	Road becomes **Davis Ave.** at curve in road near pond (on left)
0.3	22.2	**S**	At circle. Road changes name to **Indian Harbor Rd.**
0.1	22.3	**R**	**Museum Dr.** (Bruce Museum will be on the right)
0.2	22.5	**S**	Cross Steamboat Rd. at traffic light. Road becomes **Arch St.** and goes under I-95 and railroad. CAUTION: Traffic is heavy around Turnpike entrances. Obey red lights!
0.3	22.8	**L**	**Railroad Ave.** (traffic light beyond railroad underpass). Road will change name to **Old Field Point Rd., Hamilton Ave.** and **Ritch Ave.** as you ride along
1.4	24.2	**L**	Into **Byram Park**
0.1	24.3	**R**	After passing entrance booth. Ride past a small marina
0.3	24.6	**L**	**Byram Shore Rd.** (T)
1.0	25.6	**R**	**James St.**
0.2	25.8	**R**	**Mead Ave.** (T)
0.3	26.1		Return to **Mill St.** and **Mead Ave.** (end of route)

GREENWICH SAMPLER
(26.1 miles)

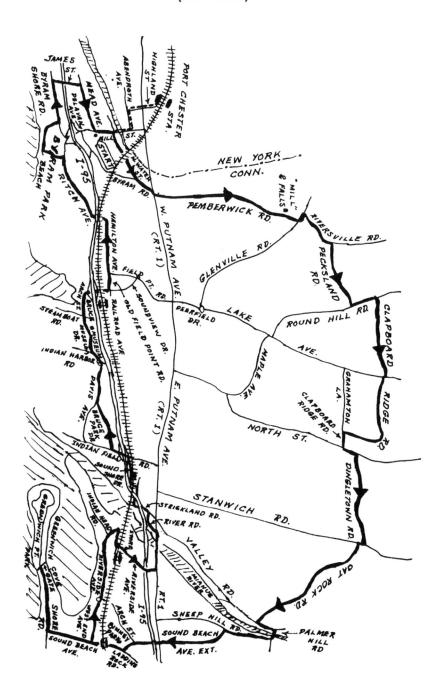

GREENWICH-ARMONK   36.2 miles

Terrain: Rolling with quite a few short but intensely steep stretches.
Traffic: For the most part, incredibly light. They don't call the northern part of Greenwich "the back country" for nothing.
Road Conditions: Excellent. One small section of dirt road.
Points of Interest: The immense wealth and beauty of **Back Country Greenwich; Museum of Cartoon Art; outdoor sculpture garden** at Pepsico; **SUNY/Purchase** campus; **Westchester Airport;** park in Armonk for picnics; **Audubon Center** of Greenwich.

Greenwich is an immense town stretching ten miles inland from Long Island Sound. The interior section contains miles of quiet, well-paved roads which pass large estates set amongst woods and fields. Don't be surprised if deer bound across your path.

Start in Byram, Greenwich's only true "working class" district. After following the Byram River inland for two miles, turn left into New York State. At the top of a very steep hill, which you may want to walk up, is a large castle containing the Museum of Cartoon Art. This museum is a must-see for any Sunday funnies fan; they occasionally have famous cartoonists as speakers.

Next head to Pepsico World Headquarters. Their fine outdoor sculpture collection is open to the public. Across the road is the campus of the State University of New York at Purchase. This school is known for its theater and dance curriculum. A broad, sunny brick plaza is located above the tunnel that you cycle under.

Continue north on King St., the road that forms the border between New York and Connecticut. You may wish to take a side trip to Westchester Airport, a very busy field that still retains that small-town look (you can watch planes take off with your nose pressed against a fence at field level).

Slice through a corner of Connecticut before re-emerging in New York. Have lunch in the pleasant town of Armonk, which has several delicatessens and a nice park, complete with an overpopulation of Canada geese.

Then turn south toward the Sound. On the way back you will pass the Audubon Center (an interesting hiking area) and a house on Brookside Dr. that is as big as any French chateau.

GREENWICH-ARMONK (continued)

Directions to Starting Point: Mead Ave. and **Mill St.** in the Byram section of Greenwich is located close to Exit 2 off I-95 (the Connecticut Turnpike). Turn left onto Delavan Ave. if exiting off northbound I-95 and right if coming off southbound I-95. In several blocks you will see a firehouse on the left. Mead Ave. is the left turn just past the firehouse, and Delavan Ave. changes its name to Mill St. at this point. Park on the street or in nearby municipal lots.

Metro-North Directions: Take a New Haven Line Stamford local to Port Chester. Carry your bike down the stairs at the front of the platform, then ride away from the tracks on Highland St. Cross Main St. (Rt. 1), then take the next left (Abendroth Ave.). At the T, turn right onto Mill St. Cross the little bridge into Connecticut, then turn left at the traffic light onto North Water St. This is the intersection at Mile 0.1 of the cue sheet.

Note: You may combine this Route (p. 59) with the Armonk-Purdys route to make a challenging 82.1-mile ride. At the fork at Mile 13.0, bear right onto Byram Rd. (no sign). Pick up the Armonk-Purdys Route at Mile 1.5, then, at the end of Armonk-Purdys Route (the intersection of Rt. 128 and Bedford Rd.), return to the Greenwich-Armonk Route at Mile 14.6.

POINT TO POINT	CUME	TURN	STREET/LANDMARK
0.0	0.0	L	Start at the corner of **Mead Ave.** and **Mill St.** While standing at the end of Mead Ave., turn **left** onto **Mill St.**
0.1	0.1	R	**North Water St.** (traffic light)
0.5	0.6	L	**Byram Rd.** (T)
0.1	0.7	R	**W. Putnam Ave./Rt. 1** (T)
0.1	0.8	L	Get in left turn lane immediately and turn into **Pemberwick Rd.**
1.2	2.0	L	**Comly Ave.** (possibly no sign). Street crosses over concrete bridge, then ascends steep hill.
0.3	2.3		Turn **right** at Magnolia Dr. for **Museum of Cartoon Art**
0.2	2.5	R	**King St.** (T)
1.7	4.2	L	**Anderson Hill Rd.** (blinking yellow light)
0.9	5.1	L	Into **Pepsico Headquarters** at traffic light
0.3	5.4		After viewing outdoor sculptures, cycle back the way you came
0.3	5.7	S	At light into **SUNY/Purchase** campus
0.1	5.8	L	**West Rd.** (T)

continued

GREENWICH-ARMONK (continued)

POINT TO POINT	CUME	TURN	STREET/LANDMARK
0.1	5.9	R	**Lincoln Ave.** (through campus)
1.1	7.0	L	At stop sign (no street sign)
0.0	7.0	R	Immediate **right** onto street with open gate. You will pass maintenance garage on your right
0.6	7.6	L	**King St.** (stop sign)
1.2	8.8		Turn **left** at Rye Lake Ave. (traffic light) for side trip to **Westchester Airport**
0.5	9.3	R	**Bedford Rd.**
2.6	11.9	L	**Riversville Rd.** (T). Proceed into New York State
0.8	12.7	R	**Rt. 22** (traffic light)
0.1	12.8	L	**Cox Ave.** (blinking light)
0.2	13.0	BL	At fork to continue on **Cox Ave.** *(Bear right here to join Armonk-Purdys Route)*
0.7	13.7	BL	At fork by cemetery after crossing I-684 to go onto **School St.** (Cox Ave. goes right)
0.3	14.0	L	**Rt. 128** (T)
0.5	14.5		Delicatessens available in the center of **Armonk**
0.1	14.6	L	**Bedford Rd.** (blinking light) *(Return from Armonk-Purdys Route)*
0.2	14.8	R	**Maple Ave.** (sto sign and red blinking light; **picnic park** is located diagonally across the street at this corner)
0.1	14.9	L	**Rt. 22** (traffic light)
0.7	15.6	R	**N. Greenwich Rd./Rt. 433** (traffic light). Road becomes **Riversville Rd.** when you re-enter Connecticut
0.8	16.4	BL	To continue on **Riversville Rd.** (Bedford Rd. goes right)
1.4	17.8	L	**John St. (Audubon Center of Greenwich** on left)
1.4	19.2	L	**Round Hill Rd.** (T)
0.8	20.0	BL	To continue on **Round Hill Rd.** (Close Rd. goes right)
2.0	22.0	S	At stop sign (Banksville Rd. goes left)
0.0	22.0	R	Immediate **right** onto **Mead Rd.**
0.4	22.4		Becomes dirt road. Pavement resumes shortly
0.3	22.7	BL	Onto **Lake Ave.** (Edgar Rd. goes right)
0.7	23.4	R	To continue on **Lake Ave.** (stop sign)

continued

GREENWICH-ARMONK (continued)

POINT TO POINT	CUME	TURN	STREET/LANDMARK
0.7	24.1	**BL**	To continue on **Lake Ave.** (Close Rd. goes right)
1.9	26.0	**L**	**Old Mill Rd.** (no sign) at stop sign after crossing Merritt Pkwy.
0.2	26.2	**R**	**Butternut Hollow Rd.** (yield sign)
0.9	27.1	**L**	**Lake Ave.** (T)
2.1	29.2	**S**	At rotary to continue on **Lake Ave.** (Round Hill Rd. goes right)
1.2	30.4	**S**	Go half way around rotary toward Greenwich Business District and onto **Dearfield Dr.**
0.4	30.8	**R**	**Rt. 1** (traffic light)
0.1	30.9	**R**	**Brookside Dr.** (next traffic light). Look for huge house on the left
0.5	31.4	**BL**	**Glenville Rd.** (T)
1.6	33.0	**L**	**Weaver St.** (by Texaco station)
1.6	34.6	**L**	**East Weaver St.** just past Greenwich Office Park
0.1	34.7	**R**	**W. Putnam Ave./Rt. 1**
0.2	34.9	**L**	**Western Junior Highway** (next light)
0.3	35.2	**R**	**Henry St.**
0.2	35.4	**BL**	At top of sudden rise to continue on **Henry St.**
0.0	35.4	**L**	**Byram Ave.** (stop sign; no street sign)
0.4	35.8	**R**	**Frontage Rd.** (T)
0.1	35.9	**R**	**Delavan Ave.** (traffic light)
0.3	36.2	**L**	Return to **Mead Ave.** and **Mill St.** (end of route)

GREENWICH-ARMONK
(36.2 miles)

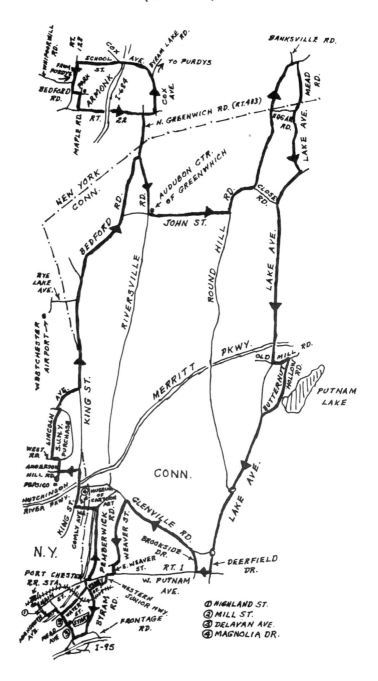

① HIGHLAND ST.
② MILL ST.
③ DELAVAN AVE.
④ MAGNOLIA DR.

RIDES STARTING IN

CENTRAL WESTCHESTER

Central Westchester is not well known as a good cycling section because it is growing rapidly and there aren't many through roads—an equation that could mean lots of traffic to contend with. Yet there are enough back roads and bike paths in this area to make for very enjoyable riding. Sleepy Hollow country has so many points of interest that occasional traffic is only a minor drawback.

Sleepy Hollow Special specializes in the landmarks of the land of Washington Irving. Tour Irving's Sunnyside mansion and the nearby Lyndhurst castle (the two are connected by a ride atop the New York City aqueduct). Then head to Phillipsburg Manor's working mill and colonial farm life exhibitions. Sleepy Hollow Cemetery and the Old Dutch Church are next, followed by Boxwood Hall (no building here, but a fantastic place to picnic on a great lawn overlooking the Hudson). Return through the Rockefeller countryside of Pocantico Hills.

White Plains-Croton Point features two of Westchester's premier bike paths, paralleling the Bronx River Pkwy. and over the old Putnam rail line. In between you ride over the Kensico Dam. Croton Point offers majestic views of the lower Hudson Highlands and is a cool spot even on a hot summer day because it sticks way out into the Hudson. On the way back you will tour the old riverside village of Ossining (passing its most famous institution, Sing Sing Prison) and head through Sleepy Hollow country and Pocantico Hills.

White Plains-Bedford connects the current county seat with a former county seat. This route is not growing as much as the area covered by the other two routes, so the roads are very quiet. En route to Bedford you ride alongside Kensico Reservoir for three miles, stop to watch the planes at the county airport, and cut through a wealthy corner of Greenwich, Conn. Eat lunch on the Bedford town green. If you think this village looks like New England, you're right—it used to be part of Connecticut. Head back via more Greenwich countryside (horse farms and art barns) and a quick tour of Usonia, a neighborhood of homes designed by Frank Lloyd Wright.

SLEEPY HOLLOW SPECIAL
(24.7 miles)

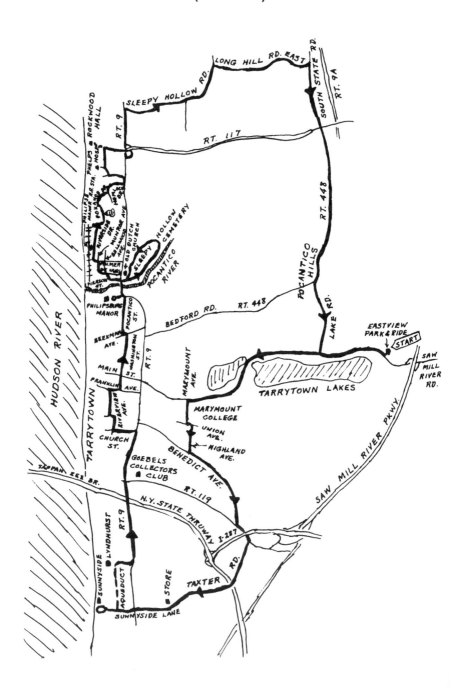

SLEEPY HOLLOW SPECIAL   24.7 miles

Terrain: Hilly, with a few memorable climbs. But some parts of the route, notably by Tarrytown Lakes and in Philipse Manor, aren't too bad!
Traffic: Fairly light, except rush hours by Tarrytown Lakes. One short run on Rt. 119 and two short stretches on Rt. 9 are busy.
Road Conditions: Mostly good. The short stretch of aqueduct riding is unpaved.
Points of Interest: Two **Sleepy Hollow Restorations: Sunnyside** (Washington Irving's home) and **Philipsburg Manor;** the **Lyndhurst Mansion; Goebel's Collectors Club; Sleepy Hollow Cemetery** and **Old Dutch Church;** scenic roads and homes in **Philipse Manor** and **Pocantico Hills.**

Many of Central Westchester's finest historic and scenic areas are incorporated in this route. The terrain makes it necessary to put a little effort into the cycling here, but most of the steeper climbs are short and on quiet roads that allow walking if necessary without interfering with auto traffic.

Ride by the lovely Tarrytown Lakes, with the towers of Marymount College in the distance. Then climb through the hilly campus before eventually emerging onto Westchester's "corporate strip," Route 119.

Head down toward the Hudson on Taxter Rd. If you like Mexican food, be sure to stop at the Brookside Grocery and Deli—the store is run by a Mexican-American family and serves fantastic homemade burritos and tacos to go.

Sunnyside, at the bottom of a nice hill, was Washington Irving's home. This is one of three restored homes run by Sleepy Hollow Restorations. You may purchase a joint ticket and visit all three. This tour passes two sites and the third, Van Cortlandt Manor, is on the two Croton routes (p. 73 and p. 77) and only a 20 minute car drive north. The tours at these restored homes are excellent; they are given by informative hosts and hostesses in period costumes.

After visiting Sunnyside, ride atop the New York City aqueduct to Lyndhurst. This 19th century mansion requires a separate admission fee.

Head to Tarrytown next (riders who like figurines may wish a short detour to the Goebel's Collectors Club). Ride through this busy village on side roads paralleling Rt. 9. Two more historic sites are located across the road from each other in North Tarrytown: Philipsburg Manor, with its working waterwheel and picturesque mill pond, and Sleepy Hollow Cemetery. The ride around the cemetery is 1.7 miles and quite beautiful, especially the road next to the Pocantico River. Be sure to stop and see the Old Dutch Church. You may wish to look for Washington Irving's grave.

The route next enters the pretty, wealthy residential section called Philipse Manor. Cyclists coming by train start here. Next, ride through Phelps Hospital roads to go to Rockwood Hall. There used to be a mansion here;

SLEEPY HOLLOW SPECIAL (continued)

although the house is gone, the beautiful lawn on a hillside overlooking the Hudson makes this an ideal lunch spot. The land is part of the Rockefeller Estate but open to the (non-motorized) public.

The final 10 miles of the route goes through Pocantico Hills, an anomaly in busy central Westchester. The reason why this section contains woods, fields, working cattle farms and a picture-perfect village rather than houses and office buildings is that most of the land is owned by the Rockefeller family. A good part of the estate has been donated to the New York State park system and is open to the public for hiking, horseback riding, cross-country skiing and mountain cycling.

Directions to Starting Point: The **Eastview Park and Ride Lot** is on Saw Mill River Rd., just west of the Saw Mill River Pkwy. Eastview exit (which is the first exit coming north from I-287). If you are coming from White Plains, exit off I-287 at the Sprain Brook Pkwy. North, then turn off at Rt. 100C. Turn left on 100C, which runs into Saw Mill River Rd. near the Union Carbide offices. (If the Park and Ride Lot is full, continue to Marymount College, where street parking is available.)
Metro-North Directions: Take a Hudson Line local train to Philipse Manor. Walk your bike onto the road adjacent to the platform, then ride north (the river and the tracks will be on your left). You are now on Riverside Dr., heading toward the turn at Mile 13.1. When you reach the end of the cue sheet, cycle back to the train station by following the route from the beginning.

POINT TO POINT	CUME	TURN	STREET/LANDMARK
0.0	0.0	**R**	Exit Eastview Park and Ride Lot and turn **right** onto unnamed road which goes by Tarrytown Lakes
1.6	1.6	**L**	At sign for **Marymount College;** ride through the campus
0.3	1.9	**L**	**Union Ave.** (stop sign)
0.1	2.0	**R**	**Highland Ave.** (stop sign; the street sign is on the left)
0.3	2.3	**L**	**Benedict Ave.** (traffic light)
1.0	3.3	**L**	**Rt. 119** (T)
0.5	3.8	**R**	**Taxter Rd.** (traffic light immediately after riding under I-287)
1.6	5.4		Road changes name to **Sunnyside Lane;** Brookside Grocery and Deli on right
0.6	6.0	**S**	At traffic light (cross Rt. 9)

SLEEPY HOLLOW SPECIAL (continued)

POINT TO POINT	CUME	TURN	STREET/LANDMARK
0.4	6.4	BR	To enter **Sunnyside,** Washington Irving's restored home
0.2	6.6		**U-turn** and head back the way you came in
0.3	6.9	L	**Bike Route** (aqueduct; unpaved)
0.6	7.5		Enter **Lyndhurst Mansion** grounds. Ride directly out to Rt. 9 if you do not wish to tour the mansion
0.2	7.7	L	**Rt. 9**
0.6	8.3		Turn **right** at Rt. 119 if you wish to go to **Goebel's Collectors Club** (which will be on your left)
0.7	9.0	L	**Church St.**
0.1	9.1	R	**Riverview Ave.**
0.1	9.2	R	To continue on **Riverview Ave.** (Bridge St. goes straight)
0.1	9.3	BL	To continue on **Riverview Ave.** (no sign)
0.1	9.4	R	At stop sign (no street sign) onto **Franklin Ave.**
0.1	9.5	L	First left (no street sign) onto **Washington St.**
0.7	10.2	L	**Beekman Ave.**
0.1	10.3	R	**Pocantico St.**
0.3	10.6	SL	**Sharp left** at light to enter **Philipsburg Manor—Upper Mills;** after touring Manor, or if you choose not to enter the manor, turn **left** onto **Rt. 9 North**
0.1	10.7	R	Into gate of **Sleepy Hollow Cemetery. Old Dutch Church of Sleepy Hollow** is on your left as you enter. Ride around the perimeter of the cemtery, first following the brook (which is on your right)
1.7	12.4	S	Exit the cemetery through the entrance you came in. Go **straight** across Rt. 9 onto **Pierson St.,** which changes name to **Bellwood Ave.**
0.2	12.6	L	**DeVries Ave.**
0.1	12.7	R	**Munroe Ave.**
0.1	12.8	L	**Palmer Ave.** (stop sign)
0.1	12.9	R	Curve right toward **Philipse Manor train station**
0.2	13.1	BL	At fork onto **Riverside Dr.** which changes name to **Pokahoe Dr.**
0.9	14.0	L	**Hemlock Dr.** (T)
0.3	14.3	L	**Rt. 9 North** (T)
0.1	14.4	L	Turn **left** immediately at traffic light toward **Phelps Memorial Hospital Center**

continued

SLEEPY HOLLOW SPECIAL (continued)

POINT TO POINT	CUME	TURN	STREET/LANDMARK
0.1	14.5	**BR**	Toward main entrance of hospital
0.2	14.7	**R**	After passing hospital's main entrance
0.1	14.8		**Rockwood Hall** entrance on left through barricade (IBM entrance is straight ahead)
0.3	15.1		If you are exiting Rockwood Hall, go **straight** toward Rts. 9 and 117. This is a **right** turn if you are not going into Rockwood Hall
0.3	15.4	**R**	Toward **Rt. 9**
0.1	15.5	**R**	**Rt. 9 North** (T)
1.1	16.6	**R**	**Sleepy Hollow Rd.**
1.3	17.9	**BL**	At fork (no street signs)
1.3	19.2	**R**	**Long Hill Rd. East.** CAUTION: in 0.6 miles, road becomes steep and curvy—control your speed!
1.1	20.3	**R**	**South State Rd.** (T)
0.8	21.1	**S**	**Rt. 448** (traffic light; cross Rt. 117)
2.4	23.5	**BL**	At fork by Pocantico Hills green onto **Lake Rd.**
0.7	24.2	**L**	At T and stop sign with Tarrytown Lakes in front of you; no street sign
0.5	24.7	**L**	Into **Eastview Park and Ride Lot** (end of route)

WHITE PLAINS-CROTON POINT   37.0 miles

Terrain: Some rather steep hills, but mostly rolling.
Traffic: Averages out to moderate. Light in Sleepy Hollow and Scarborough, heavy from Ossining to Croton Point and near Grasslands. A total of 6.4 miles of traffic-free bike path, and 0.3 miles roundtrip on a shoulderless superhighway bridge over the Croton River.
Road Conditions: Fair to good.
Points of Interest: Two of Westchester's original **bike paths** (Bronx River Pkwy. and Rt. 9A); **Croton Point Park** (picnicking, swimming, **Clearwater Folk Festival** in June); **Sing Sing Prison;** wealthy homes in **Scarborough;** the open fields of the **Rockefeller Estate** along Sleepy Hollow Rd.; **Hammond House** museum (small restored farmhouse); **Washington's Headquarters** in White Plains.

Ride from Westchester's county seat to Croton Point Park, a green peninsula jutting out into the Hudson River. The park is home to a folk music festival centered around the sloop Clearwater. The festival takes place the second or third weekend in June.

Start by cycling Westchester's original bike path, alongside the nation's original scenic parkway, the Bronx River Pkwy. At Kensico Dam, ride top the to under a canopy of shade trees on a smooth, traffic-free brick road. Then head over the dam, with excellent views of Kensico Reservoir on the right and central Westchester on the left.

Head through aptly-named Pleasantville, past Pace College, then pick up the bike path which parallels Rt. 9A. This path used to be the Putnam Division of the New York Central Railroad. Leave the path at the Briarcliff station, now the public library for that village.

Ride toward busy Ossining. The route from Ossining to Croton Point is on busy Rt. 9, and the greenhorn cyclist should note this includes a short section of well-shouldered superhighway. Traffic is generally not heavy at this point and the authors have found drivers to be courteous on the .15-mile bridge where cyclists must leave the shoulder and share the traffic lanes with cars.

Your reward for bravery is Croton Point Park, with its magnificent river views. Because the park is a peninsula and winds often blow up and down the river, Croton Point is much cooler than surrounding areas on hot summer days. If this natural air conditioning isn't enough, you may swim in the river here (county park permit may be required for beach entry).

Return up Rt. 9 for a back-roads tour of Ossining that includes a peek at infamous Sing Sing Prison. Ride through wealthy Scarborough before going inland into Sleepy Hollow country. Most of the beautiful wooded hills and open fields along Sleepy Hollow Rd. are part of the Rockefeller Estate or the new state park donated by the Rockefellers; it is open to the non-motorized public.

WHITE PLAINS-CROTON POINT (continued)

Ride back to White Plains by way of Tarrytown Lakes; under the Union Carbide building (which is built over Saw Mill River Rd.); past Hammond House museum, Grasslands Reservation (hospitals and jail) and Westchester Community College. You may wish to stop at Washington's Headquarters before the 1.8-mile ride on the bike path back to White Plains.

Directions to Starting Point: The **County Center Parking Lot** is directly off the Bronx River Pkwy., just north of downtown White Plains. Turn right if heading north on the parkway (which you cannot do by car on bicycle Sundays). From I-287, use Exit 5, then follow Rt. 100 South. The County Center is a left turn where Rt. 100 turns right onto Central Ave.

Metro-North Directions: Take a Harlem Line local or express to White Plains. Walk your bikes under the tracks. The bike path is between the railroad and the Bronx River Pkwy. Turn right on the path and proceed about one-quarter mile to the County Center Parking Lot.

Note: Cyclists wishing to add an additional 16 miles (round-trip) may start in Bronxville and use the Bronx River Valley Route (p.23) to reach White Plains. On Bicycle Sundays (see introduction to Southern Westchester section), you may ride on the parkway itself.

POINT TO POINT	CUME	TURN	STREET/LANDMARK
0.0	0.0		Exit County Center Parking Lot onto **bike path** heading north (railroad will be on your right). Path starts near the rear of the parking lot, and parallels Bronx River Pkwy.
1.0	1.0	L	Into **North White Plains station parking lot.** Do not go under railroad
0.3	1.3	L	**Fisher Lane** (at end of parking lot). Go over steel-deck bridge then turn **right** immediately onto **path.**
1.2	2.5		At end of bike path, cross busy road by Kensico Plaza park entrance. Turn **right** then **left** and ride up **brick road** to top of dam
0.4	2.9	L	At top of brick path. Ride atop Kensico Dam
1.3	4.2	R	**Columbus Ave.** (T)
2.3	6.5	BL	**Kensico Rd.**
0.7	7.2	R	**Rt. 141/Broadway** (traffic light)
1.2	8.4	L	**Bedford Rd.** (traffic light)

continued

WHITE PLAINS-CROTON POINT (continued)

POINT TO POINT	CUME	TURN	STREET/LANDMARK
0.9	9.3	S	At traffic light in downtown Pleasantville past railroad overpass. Cross Memorial Plaza and Marble Ave.
0.1	9.4	L	First turn, opposite Getty Station (no street sign) to continue on **Bedford Rd./Rt. 117.** Cross Saw Mill River Pkwy. shortly
1.1	10.5	R	Onto **bike path** after going over Rt. 9A
1.7	12.2	L	After underpass turn **left** off bike path by **Briarcliff Public Library** (old railroad station)
0.2	12.4	R	At top of library driveway (T) onto **Pleasantville Rd.** (no sign)
0.2	12.6	R	At T toward Briarcliff and Ossining, to continue on **Pleasantville Rd.** (S. State Rd. goes left)
2.0	14.6	L	**Croton Ave./Rt. 133** (T)
0.7	15.3	R	**S. Highland Ave./Rt. 9 North**
1.6	16.9	S	Continue on **Rt. 9 North** at Rt. 9A fork. CAUTION: Entering short stretch of superhighway. Be careful at Rt. 9A merge! *Walk bike* across right lane to shoulder!
0.7	17.6	R	At **Croton Pt. Ave.** exit
0.2	17.8	L	At stop sign at end of ramp
0.1	17.9	S	Traffic light—Cross one lane viaduct over railroad yards
0.5	18.4	BR	Toward **Croton Point Park**
0.7	19.1		Picnic area by the river. Return the way you came in
1.0	20.1	S	At traffic light to cross viaduct over railroad yards
0.3	20.4	R	**Rt. 9 South** entrance
0.8	21.2	S	Follow **Rt. 9** toward Tarrytown (Rt. 9A goes left)
1.8	23.0	R	**Main St.** in Ossining
0.0	23.0	BR	At fork to continue on **Main St.**
0.2	23.2	L	**State St.** (no sign). Turn is before a steep descent
0.5	23.7		**Sing Sing Prison** on right
0.1	23.8	L	**Lafayette Ave.**
0.1	23.9	R	**Spring St.**
0.4	24.3	S	At stop sign. Cross Liberty St. onto **Rockledge Ave.**
0.2	24.5	R	**Revolutionary Rd.**
0.2	24.7	R	**Kemeys Ave.** (stop sign)
0.5	25.2	BR	**River Rd.**

continued

WHITE PLAINS-CROTON POINT (continued)

POINT TO POINT	CUME	TURN	STREET/LANDMARK
0.7	25.9	**BR**	To continue on **River Rd.** (Woodlea Lane goes left)
0.1	26.0	**BR**	To continue on **River Rd.** (Creighton Lane goes left)
0.2	26.2	**R**	**Rt. 9** (T)
0.5	26.7	**L**	**Sleepy Hollow Rd.**
1.3	28.0	**R**	At fork (no signs) to continue on **Sleepy Hollow Rd.**
0.5	28.5	**R**	Curve right to continue on **Sleepy Hollow Rd.** (Old Sleepy Hollow Rd. goes left)
1.5	30.0	**BL**	At fork to continue on **Sleepy Hollow Rd.** (Webber Ave. goes straight)
0.2	30.2	**S**	At stop sign. Cross Bedford Rd. Road changes name to **County House Rd.**
0.7	30.9	**L**	T with Tarrytown Lakes in front of you
1.2	32.1	**S**	Under Union Carbide building
0.3	32.4	**L**	**Rt. 100C**
0.5	32.9		**(Hammond House** museum will be on your left in 0.5 miles)
0.6	33.5	**S**	**Rt. 100 South/Grasslands Rd.** (Rt. 100A goes right; Rt. 100 north goes left)
1.3	34.8	**L**	**Virginia Rd.** (by Shell Station)
0.4	35.2	**S**	At traffic light to cross Bronx River Pkwy.
0.0	35.2	**R**	Immediate **right** turn onto **bike path**
0.5	35.7	**L**	**Fisher Lane.** Cross steel deck bridge then turn **right** immediately into **North White Plains station parking lot**
0.3	36.0	**R**	To continue on **bike path** (tunnel under railroad is on the left)
1.0	37.0		Return to **County Center Parking Lot** (end of route)

WHITE PLAINS-CROTON POINT
(37.0 miles)

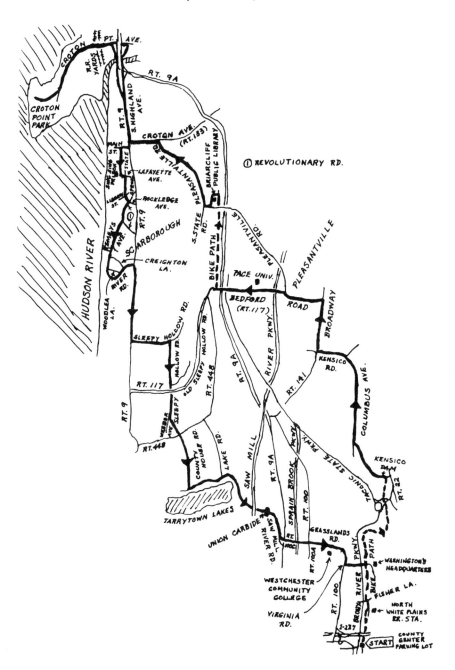

WHITE PLAINS-BEDFORD
(55.7 miles)

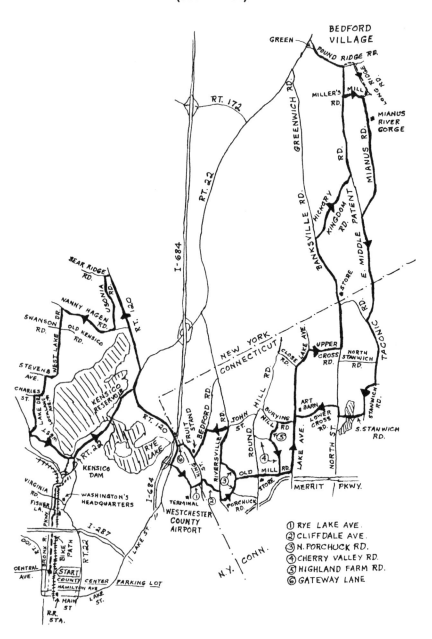

WHITE PLAINS-BEDFORD

55.7 miles

Terrain: Quite hilly throughout, but very few "killer" hills. Mostly long ascents and descents. One section of short, steep "roller coasters."
Traffic: Very light, even on Rt. 22 by Kensico Reservoir, a favorite cycling route.
Road Conditions: Excellent. One stretch of dirt road near Bedford Village (the cue sheet presents a paved alternate).
Points of Interest: Washington's Headquarters in White Plains; **Westchester Airport; backcountry Greenwich; Bedford Village** historic district and town green; **Mianus River Gorge** hiking; **Frank Lloyd Wright-designed homes** in Usonia; riding over **Kensico Dam.**

This challenging tour covers a beautiful section of Westchester and also passes through the a posh corner of backcountry Greenwich, Connecticut. The destination (Bedford Village green) is an extremely popular one among local cyclists.

Start by riding north out of White Plains along the Bronx River Pkwy. bike path. The unimposing but historically important Washington's Headquarters is located right off the path on Virginia Rd.

Head up to the top of Kensico Dam on a smooth brick road closed to autos. Cycle alongside Kensico Reservoir for three miles—look for whitecaps on the lake on windy days! Ride over to Westchester County Airport, where you can watch planes of every description take off and have a snack in the tiny terminal building.

Next, cross into Connecticut. This part of the ride features roller-coaster hills—short, steep and curvy. As you head north toward Banksville (where you re-enter New York), the hills get longer and less steep. The houses are set well back from the roads and are valued in the seven digits.

Relax on the Bedford Green and walk around the historic town. Peek into the window of the 18th century courthouse, which recalls the days when this village and White Plains were both county seats. The New Englandy look of Bedford Village is genuine, for this area was once part of Connecticut.

Those who don't mind a steep unpaved downhill can take Miller's Mill Road from the top; others may opt for the bypass. Both routes meet at the scenic mill, now a private home. Stop at Mianus River Gorge for the excellent water, which you pump yourself. Cyclists with time and energy should hike the trails here—it is a beautiful wild area with an impressively deep gorge.

Next, head back into Connecticut (the border is near a horse farm). A point of interest on the return route is the Art Barn, an interesting shop run by friendly folks who have been known to fill a cyclist's water bottle. The landmark that marks re-entry into New York is Purdy's fruit stand, which has good cider in the fall.

WHITE PLAINS-BEDFORD (continued)

At the north end of Kensico Reservoir is Usonia, an entire area of Frank Lloyd Wright homes. The "killer" hill on Nannyhagen Rd. allows you to ride back on the west side of the reservoir, then cross Kensico Dam before joining the Bronx River Pkwy. bike path for the return to White Plains.

Directions to Starting Point: The **County Center Parking Lot** is directly off the Bronx River Pkwy., just north of downtown White Plains. Turn right if heading north on the parkway (which you cannot do by car on bicycle Sundays). From I-287, use Exit 5, then follow Rt. 100 south. The County Center is a left turn where Rt. 100 turns right onto Central Ave.

Metro-North Directions: Take a Harlem Line local or express to White Plains. Walk your bikes under the tracks. The bike path is between the railroad and the Bronx River Pkwy. Turn right on the path and proceed about one-quarter mile to the County Center Parking Lot.

Note: Cyclists wishing to add an additional 16 miles (round-trip) may start in Bronxville and use the Bronx River Valley Route (p. 23) to reach White Plains. On Bicycle Sundays (see introduction to Southern Westchester section), you may ride on the parkway itself.

You may combine this route with the Bedford-Ridgefield ride (p. 65) for an especially challenging 83.2-miler. Pick up the Bedford-Ridgefield ride from its beginning at the Bedford Green, which is at Mile 24.9 of this route.

WHITE PLAINS-BEDFORD (continued)

POINT TO POINT	CUME	TURN	STREET/LANDMARK
0.0	0.0		Exit County Center Parking Lot onto **bike path** heading north (railroad will be on your right). Path starts near the rear of the parking lot, and parallels Bronx River Pkwy.
1.0	1.0	L	Into **North White Plains station parking lot.** Do not go under railroad
0.3	1.3	L	**Fisher Lane** (at end of parking lot). Go over steel-deck bridge then turn **right** immediately onto **path.**
0.5	1.8		Turn **right** on Virginia Rd. for side trip to **Washington's Headquarters**
0.7	2.5		At end of bike path, cross busy road by Kensico Plaza park entrance. Turn **right** then **left** and ride up **brick road** to top of dam
0.4	2.9	R	At top of brick path
0.1	3.0	L	**Rt. 22 North** (T)
3.1	6.1	R	**Rt. 120 South** toward Rye (traffic light)
2.0	8.1	L	**Westchester Airport** entrance road (at traffic light by I-684 entrance)
0.9	9.0	L	**Rye Lake Ave.** (by Gulf Station). Go **straight** here if you want to visit the airport terminal (water and restrooms)
0.2	9.2	L	**King St.** (traffic light at top of hill)
0.1	9.3	R	**Cliffdale Ave.** CAUTION: Intensely steep and curvy downhill, culminating in wood-floored bridge that is *extremely slippery when wet!* Keep your speed in check!
1.2	10.5	R	**Riversville Rd.** (T)
0.4	10.9	L	**Porchuck Rd.**
0.7	11.6	L	**N. Porchuck Rd.**
0.6	12.2	R	**Old Mill Rd.**
0.8	13.0	S	Cross Round Hill Rd. at stop sign. **Store** on right at intersection
1.1	14.1	L	**Lake Ave.** (T)
1.5	15.6	BR	At fork to continue on **Lake Ave.** (Close Rd. goes left)
0.6	16.2	R	**Upper Cross Rd.**
1.0	17.2	L	**North St.** (T)
1.0	18.2		**Store** on right at New York State border

continued

WHITE PLAINS-BEDFORD (continued)

POINT TO POINT	CUME	TURN	STREET/LANDMARK
2.0	20.2	R	**Hickory Kingdom Rd.**
1.9	22.1	BL	**E. Middle Patent Rd.**
2.2	24.3	L	**Pound Ridge Rd.** (T)
0.5	24.8	BR	At **Bedford Green** (toward Rt. 22 North)
0.1	24.9		Turn around at Rt. 22 and return the way you came. Stores available on the right
0.1	25.0	L	**Pound Ridge Rd./Rt. 172**
0.5	25.5	R	**Middle Patent Rd.** If you wish to avoid a steep dirt downhill, go **straight** on Rt. 172 for 0.2 miles and turn **right** toward Stamford on **Long Ridge Rd.** (no sign). In 0.6 miles, turn **right** onto **Miller's Mill Rd.** Go 0.1 mile and turn **left** onto **Mianus Rd.,** where you rejoin the main route at Mile 26.3.
0.6	26.1	L	**Miller's Mill Rd.** CAUTION: Unpaved road with steep downhill
0.2	26.3	R	**Mianus Rd.**
0.6	26.9		**Mianus River Gorge** hiking/nature area on left. Water and restrooms available
1.8	28.7	L	**East Middle Patent Rd.** (T)
2.2	30.9	L	**Taconic Rd.** (T)
1.2	32.1	S	North Stanwich Rd. goes right
0.8	32.9	BR	At "Y" onto **Stanwich Rd.**
0.3	33.2	R	**S. Stanwich Rd.** (cross lake)
0.6	33.8	R	**North St.** (T)
0.4	34.2	L	**Lower Cross Rd.**
1.5	35.7	BL	**Lake Ave.** (T) (**Art Barn** on right before intersection)
0.1	35.8	R	**Burying Hill Rd.**
0.4	36.2	L	**Highland Farm Rd.**
0.5	36.7	L	**Cherry Valley Rd.** (T)
0.7	37.4	R	**Old Mill Rd.** (T)
0.7	38.1	S	Cross Round Hill Rd. at stop sign. Store on your left at the intersection
0.8	38.9	R	**N. Porchuck Rd.** (T)
0.5	39.4	R	**Riversville Rd.** (stop sign)
0.4	39.8	L	**John St.**
0.7	40.5	L	**Bedford Rd.** (T)
1.1	41.6	R	**King St.** (T) **Fruit stand** on right after turn

continued

WHITE PLAINS-BEDFORD (continued)

POINT TO POINT	CUME	TURN	STREET/LANDMARK
0.5	42.1	L	**Rt. 120A/Gateway Lane**
0.2	42.3	R	**Rt. 120 North** (T)
1.5	43.8	S	Continue on **Rt. 120 North** at junction of Rt. 22
0.4	44.2	L	At traffic light to continue on **Rt. 120 North**
1.9	46.1	L	**Bear Ridge Rd.**
0.1	46.2	L	**Usonia Rd.** (Frank Lloyd Wright homes)
0.9	47.1	R	**Nanny Hagen Rd.** (T)
1.2	48.3	L	**West Lake Dr.** (first left turn after "hill" sign)
0.3	48.6	S	At stop sign, crossing Swanson Rd. and Old Kensico Rd.
1.3	49.9	L	To continue on **Westlake Dr.** (Stevens Ave.goes straight)
0.2	50.1	R	To continue on **Westlake Dr.** (Lockland Ave. goes left)
0.1	50.2	L	To continue on **Westlake Dr.** (Charles St. goes straight)
1.0	51.2	L	**Columbus Ave.** (T)
0.1	51.3	L	**Westlake Dr.**
0.8	52.1		**Hot dog stand** on your right just before crossing dam
0.5	52.6	R	Onto **brick road** (starts just past the second dam pillar)
0.4	53.0	S	Cross busy road onto paved **bike path** which goes left to parallel road under an underpass, and then turns sharply right after the underpass toward the Bronx River Pkwy.
1.2	54.2	L	**Fisher Lane** (T). Cross steel deck bridge
0.0	54.2	R	Immediate **right** into **North White Plains station parking lot**
0.3	54.7	R	To continue on **path**
1.0	55.7		**County Center Parking Lot** (end of route)

RIDES STARTING IN

NORTHERN WESTCHESTER

Pedalers who ride frequently in the county usually head for Northern Westchester because it is big and open and quite a bit of it is still sparsely developed. We have the thirsty souls of New York City to thank for that, because much of the northern part of the county is taken up by the Croton watershed. As a result, you'll be riding through the woods much of the time in this section. Bring your best pair of quadriceps to the starting points: you will encounter hills.

Armonk-Purdys roughly follows the route of Interstate 684, but you will be using remote back roads out of earshot of the big highway. Along the way are several fine nature perserves, country stores, an elephant atop a pedestal, and Reader's Digest headquarters. The main attraction of this and other Northern Westchester rides are miles of traffic-free back roads in the woods and alongside reservoirs.

New England plays a major role in shaping the scenery along the **Bedford-Ridgefield** route. Bedford used to be in Connecticut, and Ridgefield still is. The stone walls and rocky terrain of everywhere from Massachusetts to Maine are in abundance in Pound Ridge, N.Y., and vicinity. Look for large, modern homes of unique design hiding deep in wooded lots.

Like to eat fruit and drink wine? Then you'll enjoy **Katonah-North Salem,** which passes an orchard and a vineyard. This pedal also features Ward Pound Ridge Reservation, the county's largest park, and Caramoor, a mansion known for its concerts and formal gardens.

Two rides leave from the convenient Croton-Harmon rail station, and directions are given to combine them into one longer route. **Croton-Mohansic** heads to Mohansic Lake in Franklin D. Roosevelt State Park by way of Croton Dam and a pick-your-own orchard on top of a challenging hill. On the way back, be sure to visit Teatown Reservation, an excellent nature preserve with a lake and museum. **Croton To The Point** visits the little-known village of Verplanck. Excellent river views can be seen here and for those interested, there's an energy exhibit at the nearby Indian Point nuclear plant. Enroute to "the Point," stop at Blue Mountain Reservation for a swim at the small lake beach.

Either Croton ride is convenient for a visit to Van Cortlandt Manor, the home of 18th Century Westchester aristocracy.

Finally, if you wish to tour extreme northwestern Westchester (and well up into Putnam County), head for the **Peekskill Hollow Ride.** This route follows narrow river valleys through remote sections of Putnam, aiming for Clarence Fahnestock Park with its excellent beach and picnic areas. On the way back you pass Westchester's only water slide in Sprout Brook Park.

ARMONK-PURDYS   49.0 miles

Terrain: Considering this is northern Westchester, not too bad. Mostly rolling, a few steep climbs. The return trip, however, contains some memorable ascents on Crow Hill Rd., Rt. 133 and Whippoorwill Rd.
Traffic: Very light, except moderate between Purdys and Somers and on Rt. 133.
Road Conditions: Very good, except dirt on Old Roaring Brook Rd.
Points of Interest: Butler and Westmoreland Sanctuaries (hiking, nature study); **Caramoor** (museum, garden, concerts); Thompson's Store in **Purdys** (an old-fashioned **general store** friendly to cyclists); the **Somers Elephant; Reader's Digest headquarters** (tour with artworks open to public on weekdays); **Whippoorwill Rd. area** (beautiful homes and views).

It is possible to drive from Armonk to Purdys in under 20 minutes on Interstate 684. A much better way to travel between these two towns is on two wheels, exploring the many quiet back roads in this affluent, still lightly settled area.

Start in Armonk, a pleasant town of shops that is home to IBM's world headquarters. Head north on roads that parallel I-684, but are generally not within earshot of the highway. Two excellent nature preserves, Butler and Westmoreland Sanctuaries, are located six miles into the route.

The next point of interest is Caramoor. This mansion is known for its formal gardens, concerts and house tour. Continue north on numbered highways which are remarkably free of traffic. Ride along pretty Titicus Reservoir into tiny Purdys. The store here has a front porch ideal for eating lunch, and is a frequent destination of local cyclists.

The return route takes you by a large pedestal in Somers, atop which is a statue of an elephant. This town is considered a birthplace of the circus in this country. Hachaliah Bailey, whose descendents later joined with Barnum, owned the hotel on the corner here, named in honor of his elephant Bet, which was the first elephant in the U.S.

Enjoy quiet backroads in the region of New York City's Croton watershed as you ride by Amawalk and Croton reservoirs. A few climbs and descents later (one of which, on Old Roaring Brook Rd., requires caution due to lack of pavement!), cycle by Reader's Digest headquarters. This imposing colonial structure contains exhibits open to the public on weekdays.

The final stretch of this route is over Whippoorwill Rd. This is definitely hilly, but the views, open fields, woods, and wealthy homes make the exertion worthwhile.

ARMONK-PURDYS (continued)

Directions to Starting Point: The ride begins at the intersection of **Rt. 128 and Bedford Rd.** in the center of Armonk. Take I-684 to Exit 3, then Rt. 22 South to the second traffic light and turn right. Parking is available on the streets of Armonk or in municipal lots.

Metro-North Directions: (Approx. 6 miles each way from station to start of ride): Take a Harlem Division local or express to White Plains North. Exit onto Fisher Lane and turn right. Ride to Rt. 22 and turn left. Follow Rt. 22 to Rt. 128 and turn left. The ride begins in several blocks at the intersection of Bedford Rd.

Note: It is possible to combine this route with the Greenwich-Armonk ride (p. 33) to make a challenging 82.1-mile circuit. See the note following the description of the Greenwich-Armonk route for the best directions.

POINT TO POINT	CUME	TURN	STREET/LANDMARK
0.0	0.0		From the intersection of Rt. 128 and Bedford Rd., ride north on **Rt. 128**
0.6	0.6	R	**School St.**
0.9	1.5	SL	**Byram Rd.** (no sign; Sunset Rd. goes off to the right beyond the turn) *(riders from Greenwich join here)*
2.5	4.0	R	**Baldwin Rd.** (no sign; turn at a road which immediately goes under I-684 and climbs a hill)
0.4	4.4	L	**Rt. 22** (T)
0.1	4.5	L	**Chestnut Ridge Rd.**
1.5	6.0	S	Road to **Butler Sanctuary** goes left. **Westmoreland Sanctuary** is on the right
1.3	7.3	L	**Rt. 172** (T)
0.9	8.2	R	**W. Patent Rd.**
0.8	9.0	S	Cross Guard Hill Rd.
0.8	9.8	L	**Broad Brook Rd.** (T)
0.1	9.9	R	**Springhurst Rd.**
0.6	10.5	R	**Bedford Center Rd.** (T)
2.6	13.1	L	At fork onto **Rt. 22** (no sign) (Bedford Cross sign is on the island of the fork)
1.5	14.6	R	**Girdle Ridge Rd.**
0.5	15.1	R	**Pea Pond Rd.** (T) (no sign)

continued

ARMONK-PURDYS (continued)

POINT TO POINT	CUME	TURN	STREET/LANDMARK
0.2	15.3		**Caramoor Center for Music and the Arts** on the right
2.0	17.3	L	**Rt. 121/Old Post Rd.** (T)
2.4	19.7	R	To continue on **Rt. 121/35 East** (T). **Deli** on left after turn
0.6	20.3	L	To continue on **Rt. 121 North** (traffic light; Rt. 35 goes straight)
2.6	22.9	S	Cross Rt. 138
0.7	23.6	BL	**Bogtown Rd.** Road changes name to **Mills Rd.**
2.5	26.1	BL	At unmarked fork to continue on **Mills Rd.**
0.4	26.5	L	**Main St.** (T) (no sign; Thompson's **Store** on right after turn)
0.1	26.6	R	**Rt. 22** (T)
0.0	26.6	L	Immediate **left** onto **Rt. 116 West**
1.5	28.1	BL	**Rt. 202 West/Rt. 100 South** (stop sign)
0.3	28.4	BR	At fork to continue on **Rt. 202** (note **elephant** in island!)
1.4	29.8	L	**Brick Hill Rd.**
0.5	30.3	R	**Rt. 139** (at fork and stop sign)
0.1	30.4	L	**Rt. 202 West**
0.6	31.0	L	**Lake Rd.** (first left after Lincoln Hall)
1.8	32.8	L	**Orchard Hill Rd.** (road goes up hill immediately)
1.5	34.3	R	**Rt. 35** (T)
0.3	34.6	L	**Wood St.**
1.5	36.1	L	**Moseman Ave.** (T)
0.7	36.8	R	**Rt. 100** (T)
1.9	38.7	S	At traffic light to continue on **Rt. 100 South.** Cross bridge over reservoir
0.4	39.1	L	At end of bridge (no sign)
0.1	39.2	R	**Crow Hill Rd.**
1.8	41.0	R	**Rt. 133** (T)
0.5	41.5	L	**Old Roaring Brook Rd.**
0.6	42.1		Road turns to dirt. Caution on downhill stretches
1.3	43.4	L	Turn toward the traffic light and cross Saw Mill River Pkwy. heading toward the Reader's Digest building

continued

ARMONK-PURDYS (continued)

POINT TO POINT	CUME	TURN	STREET/LANDMARK
0.2	43.6	**R**	**Roaring Brook Rd.** (turn is in front of the Reader's Digest building)
0.4	44.0	**R**	**Rt. 117** (T) (traffic light; no street sign)
0.4	44.4	**L**	**Whippoorwill Rd.**
2.1	46.5	**S**	At Whippoorwill Crossing. Enjoy a nice view!
1.5	48.0	**L**	**Whippoorwill Rd. East**
0.9	48.9	**R**	**Rt. 128** (traffic light)
0.1	49.0		Intersection of **Rt. 128** and **Bedford Rd.** (end of route)

ARMONK-PURDYS
(49.0 miles)

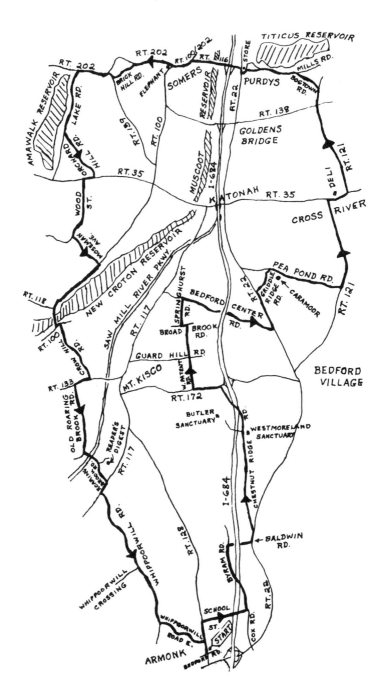

BEDFORD-RIDGEFIELD
(27.5 miles)

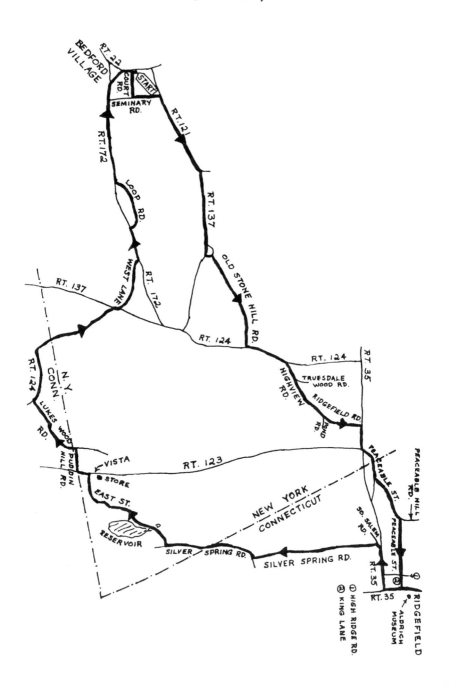

BEDFORD-RIDGEFIELD   27.5 miles

Terrain: Rolling. A few hills, but nothing that most cyclists will have trouble with.

Traffic: Light, except moderate near Ridgefield.

Road Conditions: Excellent, with some bumpy pavement near Ridgefield and about 0.8 miles of dirt road.

Points of Interest: Historic **Bedford Village;** New Englandy **Ridgefield** (large homes, Aldrich Museum and nice shops); a very quiet corner of Westchester to ride in.

The towns of Pound Ridge and Lewisboro occupy much of the land in the zigzag border between New York and Connecticut—land that was once part of New England but now is Westchester territory.

The New England influence is seen in the stone walls that abound in the woods. These walls once separated farm fields, before forests and wealthy homes took over. Cyclists will be especially impressed with the amount of rock visible on the appropriately named Old Stone Hill Rd.

Ridgefield is a "real" New England town with large, stately homes and a collection of shops catering to a well-to-do clientele. There is only one sit-down eatery in town (a coffee shop located off of Main Street to the right beyond town hall, on Bailey Ave.), but there are several delicatessens and a cart called Le Hot Dog for al fresco dining.

Return via the miniature hamlet of Vista on the New York-Connecticut state line, then through Pound Ridge, which has street signs that look like pointing arms. Be sure to walk around Bedford Village, which has numerous historic homes and an 18th-century courthouse and museum.

Directions to Starting Point: Bedford Village is in northeastern Westchester County. Take Exit 4 off I-684, then follow Rt. 172 East to Rt. 22 North. Turn right on Court St., just beyond the Bedford Village green, and park beyond the 2-hour parking signs.

Metro-North Directions: (About 7 miles each way from the station). Take a Harlem Division train bound for Brewster North to the Mt. Kisco station. Cycle east to Main St., then south on Rt. 117 to Rt. 172. Ride east on 172 to Rt. 22, then north to Bedford Village. Note that traffic can be heavy on Rt. 172.

Note: you can combine this route with the White Plains-Bedford ride for a challenging 83.2-mile trek. See the note after the White Plains-Bedford ride (p.51) for best directions.

BEDFORD-RIDGEFIELD (continued)

POINT TO POINT	CUME	TURN	STREET/LANDMARK
0.0	0.0		Start at the intersection of Court Rd. and Rt. 22. Ride on **Court Rd.** away from Rt. 22
0.3	0.3	L	**Seminary Rd.** (T)
0.2	0.5	R	**Rt. 121** (T)
1.4	1.9	R	**Rt. 137 South**
2.0	3.9	L	**Old Stone Hill Rd.**
0.0	3.9	BR	At fork immediately after last turn to continue on **Old Stone Hill Rd.**
1.7	5.6	L	**Rt. 124** (T)
1.0	6.6	R	**Highview Rd.**
0.3	6.9	BR	At fork. Truesdale Wood Road goes left
1.0	7.9	S	At stop sign (Pond Rd. goes right). Name of the road you are on changes to **Ridgefield Rd.**
0.6	8.5	R	**Rt. 35** (stop sign)
0.3	8.8	L	**Peaceable St.** (Rt. 123 goes right at this intersection)
0.3	9.1	L	Turn beyond Pinchbeck Bros. Florist to continue on **Peaceable St.** (Street sign says "Old S. Salem Rd.")
0.6	9.7	R	At first intersection to stay on **Peaceable St.** Peaceable Hill Rd. goes straight
1.0	10.7	BR	Cross High Ridge Rd. You are now on **King Lane**
0.2	10.9	L	**Rt. 35 North** (T). **Aldrich Museum of Contemporary Art** on right after turn
0.5	11.4		Turn around at the end of the downtown section and cycle back on **Rt. 35 South**
0.8	12.2	R	To continue on **Rt. 35 South**
0.8	13.0	L	**South Salem Rd.** (green sign at the intersection points right for New York)
0.0	13.0	L	**Silver Spring Rd.**
1.4	14.4	R	Continue on **Silver Spring Rd.** (T; no sign)
2.0	16.4		Road turns to dirt upon entering New York State
0.2	16.6	R	**East St.** (first right turn after road becomes dirt)
0.6	17.2		Pavement returns
1.6	18.8	L	**Rt. 123** (T). If you wish to go to a **store,** turn **right** here instead and ride about one block. Store is on the right
0.1	18.9	R	**Puddin Hill Rd.**
0.3	19.2	L	**Lukes Wood Rd.** (T; no sign). West Rd. goes right

continued

BEDFORD-RIDGEFIELD (continued)

POINT TO POINT	CUME	TURN	STREET/LANDMARK
1.0	20.2	**R**	**Rt. 124** (T)
2.9	23.1	**BR**	**Rt. 137**
0.0	23.1	**L**	Immediate **left** onto **West Lane**
0.8	23.9	**L**	**Rt. 172** (T; no sign)
1.1	25.0	**R**	**Loop Rd.**
0.5	25.5	**R**	**Rt. 172** (T; no sign)
1.9	27.4	**R**	At Bedford Green onto **Rt. 22**
0.1	27.5		Ride ends at intersection of **Court Rd.** and **Rt. 22**

KATONAH-NORTH SALEM
(33.4 miles)

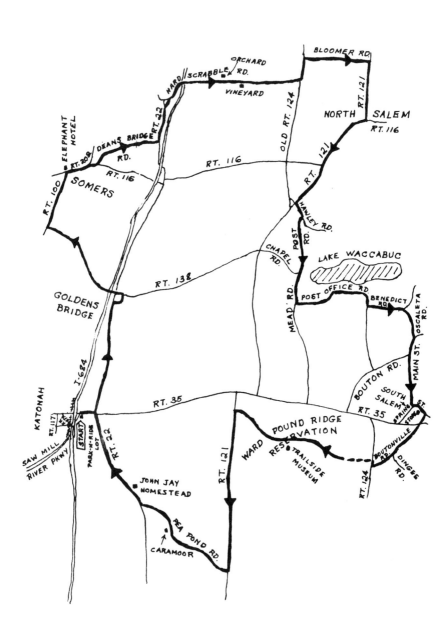

KATONAH-NORTH SALEM   33.4 miles

Terrain: Rolling, at times quite steeply. Expect some long ascents and descents.
Traffic: Light, except for the first and last 0.3 miles on Rt. 35.
Road Conditions: Excellent, when paved. Expect about a mile of dirt roads, including a steep dirt climb on Post Rd.
Points of Interest: Quiet roads and **fantastic vistas** of North and South Salem; **Waccabuc** post office, the smallest in the U.S.; a **vineyard** and **pick-your-own orchard** on Hardscrabble Rd.; **Ward Pound Ridge Reservation** (hiking, picnics and trailside museum); **Caramoor** (gardens, museum and concerts); **John Jay Homestead.**

The northeast corner of Westchester, while growing due to the presence of I-684, is still lightly settled and contains delightful riding. There are hills here, but who can forget the sight of Lake Waccabuc nestled in the valley? Your legs will forgive you.

Ride out of busy Katonah and head north for Goldens Bridge and Somers. Look for the elephant on the pedestal in Somers; this was where the first circus in the U.S. was organized. The statue was put up by Hachaliah Bailey. Next head up toward Croton Falls. For the lovers of fruit and fruits of the vine, Hardscrabble Rd. has Outhouse Orchards (so named because the owner is Mr. Outhouse) and the North Salem Vineyard.

After passing through North Salem, head toward South Salem by way of Waccabuc. That tiny building on Post Office Rd. is one of the smallest post offices in the country. Buy some food at the store in South Salem, and ride several miles further to Ward Pound Ridge Reservation for a picnic. This is Westchester's largest and most beautiful park, with many miles of wooded hilltop and streamside hiking trails and an excellent trailside museum.

Return to Katonah by way of Caramoor (a museum noted for its concerts and beautiful garden) and the home of John Jay, our first Supreme Court Chief Justice.

Directions to Starting Point: Katonah is located at the junction of I-684 and NY 35. Drivers coming from the Tappan Zee Bridge may use the Saw Mill River Pkwy. to reach I-684. Use Exit 6 and park at a dirt park and ride lot on the right at the top of the ramp, where the route begins.
Metro-North Directions: Take a Harlem Division train bound for Brewster North to the Katonah station. Proceed left (west) one block to Rt. 117. Ride right (north) to Rt. 35, then turn right on Rt. 35 East. The route begins after Rt. 35 crosses over I-684.

KATONAH-NORTH SALEM (continued)

POINT TO POINT	CUME	TURN	STREET/LANDMARK
0.0	0.0	**R**	From the parking lot at the to of the northbound exit ramp of I-684 for Rt. 35, turn **right** on **Rt. 35 East**
0.3	0.3	**L**	**Rt. 22 North** (traffic light)
2.1	2.4	**R**	Toward **Rt. 138** (by A&P shopping center)
0.2	2.6	**L**	**Rt. 138** (T)
1.9	4.5	**R**	**Rt. 100 North** (T)
0.9	5.4	**R**	At fork to continue on **Rt. 100 North/Rt. 202 East** (note **elephant** statue in island!)
0.3	5.7	**R**	**Rt. 116 East**
0.1	5.8	**L**	**Deans Bridge Rd.** (Rt. 116 curves right)
1.3	7.1	**L**	**Rt. 22** (T)
0.5	7.6	**R**	**Hardscrabble Rd.** (fork; no sign; follow signs for I-684. Rt. 22 goes left). **Vineyard** and **Orchard** will be about one mile after this intersection.
3.5	11.1	**L**	At "Y" onto **Old Rt. 124**
0.4	11.5	**R**	**Bloomer Rd.**
1.3	12.8	**R**	**Rt. 121** (T)
1.2	14.0	**BR**	At T, to continue on **Rt. 121**
1.1	15.1	**BL**	At fork to continue on **Rt.121 South** (Rt. 116 goes right)
0.9	16.0	**L**	**Hawley Rd.** (toward Mountain Lakes Camp)
0.1	16.1	**R**	**Post Rd.**
0.2	16.3		Road becomes dirt
0.4	16.7		Pavement returns. Road changes name to **Mead St.**
1.6	18.3	**L**	**Post Office Rd.** One of the smallest post offices in the U.S. is on the right after the turn.
1.0	19.3	**L**	**Benedict Rd.**
0.8	20.1	**R**	At "Y" and yield sign onto **Oscaleta Rd.** (no street sign)
0.6	20.7	**R**	**Main St.** (T)
1.1	21.8	**BL**	**Spring St.** (stop sign)
0.1	21.9		**Store** on right
0.2	22.1	**R**	**Boutonville Rd.**
0.1	22.2	**S**	Cross Rt. 35
0.5	22.7	**S**	Road becomes dirt
0.5	23.2	**BR**	At fork to continue on **Boutonville Rd.** (Dingee Rd. goes left)
0.1	23.3	**S**	Pavement returns

continued

KATONAH-NORTH SALEM (continued)

POINT TO POINT	CUME	TURN	STREET/LANDMARK
0.2	23.5	**R**	**Rt. 124** (T)
0.1	23.6	**L**	At first paved road into **Ward Pound Ridge Reservation** (not a car entrance). Walk bike around pillars with chain across and ride into park.
1.3	24.9		**Trailside Museum** on left
1.4	26.3	**L**	**Rt. 121** (T)
2.4	28.7	**R**	**Pea Pond Rd.**
2.0	30.7		**Caramoor Center for Music and the Arts** on the left
0.6	31.3	**BR**	At yield sign onto **Rt. 22 North**
0.2	31.5		**John Jay Homestead** on right
1.6	33.1	**L**	**Rt. 35 West** (traffic light)
0.3	33.4	**L**	Into **parking lot** by I-684 northbound exit ramp. CAUTION: Walk turn! (end of route)

CROTON-MOHANSIC
(34.0 miles)

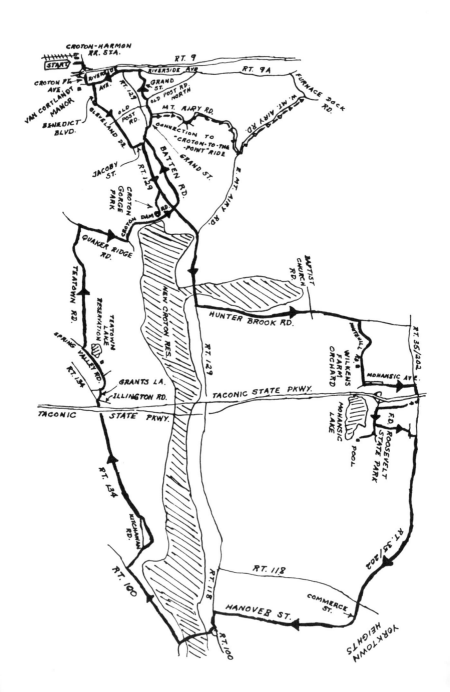

CROTON-MOHANSIC   34.0 miles

Terrain: Rolling, with a few extremely steep hills.
Traffic: Moderate near Croton, moderate to heavy on Rt. 202 into Yorktown, otherwise light.
Road Conditions: Very good.
Points of Interest: Croton Gorge Park underneath the huge Croton Dam; **Wilkens Farm** pick-your-own apples (fall); **F.D. Roosevelt (Mohansic) Park** (swimming and boating); **Teatown Lake Reservation** (hiking and nature museum); **Van Cortlandt Manor** (a Sleepy Hollow restoration).

Two of the more challenging climbs in Westchester are included in this route, yet novice cyclists should not reject this ride because overall the terrain is merely "rolling." The western end of the Croton Reservoir watershed contains some beautiful wooded and quiet back roads, and the two bad ascents can easily be walked since there is little traffic at those points.

Start by cycling out of Croton up quiet, residential streets. Take a short detour into Croton Gorge Park to see the Croton Dam, an impressive concrete structure worth a photograph if a lot of water is flowing over the spillway. Cross the reservoir, then head north along an arm of the lake on quiet Hunter Brook Rd. Turn right to climb Big Hill No. 1. The sound of a stream down in the ravine is soothing during the struggle against gravity. Reward yourself at the top with fresh fruit at Wilkens Farm if you are riding in the fall.

Next head over to F.D. Roosevelt Park, where you can picnic on a meadow overlooking Mohansic Lake, rent a boat, or swim in the pool. Ride through busy Yorktown Heights, then head up Hanover St. past one of Westchester's few working dairy farms.

The route then returns to the Croton Reservoir, crossing it on Rt. 100. The next stop is Teatown Lake Reservation, a beautiful nature preserve with an interesting museum. The roads in this section are virtually traffic-free, which is a good thing because you must climb Big Hill No. 2. This ascent is much shorter than No. 1, but quite a bit steeper. On top you will enjoy a ride down a European-looking one-lane road past lovely backwoods suburban homes and horse farms. You will emerge on top of Croton dam and only 4½ miles from the end of the route.

Van Cortlandt Manor, a Sleepy Hollow restoration, is located near the Croton-Harmon station. You may buy a combined ticket that will admit you to Sunnyside and Philipsburg Manor, located on the Sleepy Hollow Special route (p. 41).

Directions to Starting Point: The Croton-Harmon railroad station is located off Rt. 9, north of Ossining. Take the Croton Point Ave. exit. Turn left if coming off northbound Route 9 and right if coming off southbound Route 9. The station parking lot is on the left.

CROTON-MOHANSIC (continued)

Metro-North Directions: Take a Hudson Line local or express train to Croton-Harmon. The ride begins at the top of the road exiting from the station parking lot.

Note: The cue sheet includes a link to the Croton To The Point Route (p. 77). Following this link, you can have a 54.4-mile ride. The link (Mt. Airy Rd.) goes up-up-up, then down-down-down, but the bad hills fade away eventually as you get into the Croton To The Point ride and settle into a more moderate roll.

POINT TO POINT	CUME	TURN	STREET/LANDMARK
0.0	0.0	**R**	From the top of the hill at the exit from the Croton-Harmon railroad station parking lot, turn **right** onto **Croton Point Ave.**
0.2	0.2	**L**	**S. Riverside Ave.** (T; no sign)
0.1	0.3	**R**	**Benedict Blvd.**
0.2	0.5	**L**	At traffic circle, onto **Cleveland Dr.**
0.7	1.2	**S**	At stop sign, to continue on **Cleveland Dr.** Cross Old Post Rd.; Radnor Rd. goes left. You will have a cemetery on your left after passing this intersection.
0.6	1.8	**L**	**Jacoby St.**
0.1	1.9	**R**	**Rt. 129** (T)
1.0	2.9	**R**	Into **Croton Gorge Park**
0.3	3.2		**U-turn** in parking lot at the foot of the dam and ride back up the way you came.
0.3	3.5	**R**	**Rt. 129** (T)
1.9	5.4	**L**	**Hunter Brook Rd.** (just past bridge over reservoir; there may be no street sign during construction of a new bridge)
2.0	7.4	**S**	Cross Baptist Church Rd.
1.5	8.9	**R**	**Whitehill Rd.** (turn is at bottom of hill after crossing a stone bridge). You will soon begin climbing a long, very steep hill.

CROTON-MOHANSIC (continued)

POINT TO POINT	CUME	TURN	STREET/LANDMARK
0.7	9.6		**Wilkens Farm** (pick your own apples) on right
0.2	9.8	L	**Mohansic Ave.** (stop sign; second left turn at intersection)
0.9	10.7	R	**Rts. 35/202** (T)
0.3	11.0	R	Before bus shelter (after crossing under Taconic Pkwy.), walk bike around wooden barricade to enter **F.D. Roosevelt State Park.** Pedal down park road paralleling Taconic Pkwy.
0.7	11.7	BL	At fork, toward **pool.** You will pass the nicest lunch spot (a meadow overlooking Mohansic Lake, near the boathouse) on this leg.
0.5	12.2	BR	At fork, toward **pool**
0.2	12.4		**Pool** bathhouse. **U-turn,** and ride back the way you came.
0.1	12.5	BL	At fork, toward **picnic area**
0.4	12.9	R	Toward **Commercial Vehicle Exit**
0.7	13.6	BR	At fork, toward **Commercial Vehicle Exit**
0.1	13.7	L	Toward **Commercial Vehicle Exit**
0.2	13.9	R	**Rt. 35/202** toward Yorktown Heights
2.3	16.2	S	At traffic light, onto **Commerce St.** (no street sign)
0.4	16.6	S	Road name changes to **Hanover St.** as you leave the center of Yorktown Heights
3.1	19.7	L	**Rt. 118** (T)
0.2	19.9	R	At traffic circle, onto **Rt. 100 South** (toward Millwood). Cross an old reservoir bridge immediately.
0.4	20.3	R	Curve **right** after the bridge to continue on Rt. 100 South.
1.4	21.7	R	**Rt. 134**

CROTON-MOHANSIC (continued)

POINT TO POINT	CUME	TURN	STREET/LANDMARK
0.9	22.6	R	**Kitchawan Rd.**
0.5	23.1	R	**Rt. 134** (T)
0.9	24.0	BR	**Grants Lane** (first turn after Taconic Pkwy. underpass; Illington Rd. is the sharp right)
0.1	24.1	R	**Spring Valley Rd.** (T) (no street sign; sign for Teatown Reservation)
0.6	24.7	BL	To continue on **Spring Valley Rd.** (Blinn Rd. goes left)
0.1	24.8		**Teatown Reservation** on right
0.6	25.4	R	**Teatown Rd.** (no sign; first right turn after passing lake on right. Climb ridiculously steep hill immediately)
1.8	27.2	R	**Quaker Ridge Rd.** (T; no sign)
1.3	28.5	L	**Croton Dam Rd.** (no sign; turn is at a fork with a big red house directly in front of you)
0.9	29.4	S	Cross Rt. 129 onto **Batten Rd.**
1.4	30.8	R	**Rt. 129** (T)
0.3	31.1	R	**Grand St.**
0.2	31.3		*Turn **right** onto **Mt. Airy Rd.** if you are riding the joint 54.4-mile route out of Croton. See directions below. Go **straight** here to continue the 33-mile Croton-Mohansic route.*
0.2	31.5	BL	At St. Augustine's Church to continue on **Grand St.** (no sign; Old Post Rd. North goes right; turn is first left past traffic light in Croton)
0.5	32.0	L	**Riverside Ave.** (T)
0.8	32.8	R	**Croton Point Ave.** (toward railroad station). Go **straight** at this intersection if you wish to visit **Van Cortlandt Manor**
0.2	33.0	L	Into **Croton-Harmon railroad station parking lot**

DIRECTIONS FOR LINK TO CROTON TO THE POINT RIDE:

	31.3	*R*	*Mt. Airy Rd.*
0.5	*31.8*	*L*	*Curve **left** to continue on **Mt. Airy Rd.** (Riverview, Mountain and Park Trails go right)*
0.8	*32.6*	*L*	*W. Mt. Airy Rd. (T)*
1.4	*34.0*	*R*	*Furnace Dock Rd. (yield sign)*

You are now on the Croton to the Point Route. Continue on that route's cue sheet.

CROTON TO THE POINT   24.7 miles

Terrain: Moderately rolling. One extended climb (Furnace Dock Rd.).
Traffic: Moderate, with light traffic up Furnace Dock Rd. and Maple Ave., out on "the Point" and near Crugers.
Road Conditions: Good, but the roads are occasionally treated with oil and stones, which makes for somewhat messy cycling.
Points of Interest: Blue Mountain Reservation (swimming and hiking); **Indian Point energy exhibit;** good views of the Hudson at **Verplanck** and **Georges Island Park; Van Cortlandt Manor** (a Sleepy Hollow restoration).

Maps of the Hudson Valley drawn in the 18th Century call the large peninsula jutting out into the river north of Croton, Verplanck's Point. Newer maps and the Consolidated Edison people call it Indian Point. Many locals refer to it simply as "the Point." Whatever you call it, this area of little known villages and nice river views makes for good cycling.

Start by heading north out of Croton on Riverside Ave. Several nice river views are available before you turn inland (and uphill) on Furnace Dock Rd. Cycle through pleasant wooded countryside before heading back down toward the river and through a residential corner of Peekskill.

Blue Mountain Reservation is well worth a stop for its clean lake beach, picnic areas and hiking trails. Next, head toward the Indian Point nuclear generating plant. Con Edison runs an energy exhibit here that is open 10:00 a.m. to 5:00 p.m. Tues.-Sat. Enter at the main gate.

Past the nuclear plant is the quiet village of Verplanck. Enjoy the river views here and at Georges Island Park in nearby Montrose, which has excellent picnic facilities.

Cycle into quiet Crugers and through a huge chunk of undeveloped parkland (Oscawana Park) with more excellent river views before returning to Croton-Harmon. You might wish to stop at the restored Van Cortlandt Manor near the end of the tour.

Directions to Starting Point: The **Croton-Harmon railroad station** is located off Rt. 9, north of Ossining. Take the Croton Point Ave. exit. Turn left if coming off northbound Route 9 and right if coming off southbound Route 9. The station parking lot is on the left.
Metro-North Directions: Take a Hudson Line local or express train to Croton-Harmon. The ride begins at the top of the road exiting from the station parking lot.
Note: Cyclists wishing a longer ride may combine this route with the Croton-Mohansic ride (p. 73). See the Croton-Mohansic cue sheet and description for information on a 54.4-mile combined route.

CROTON TO THE POINT
(24.7 miles)

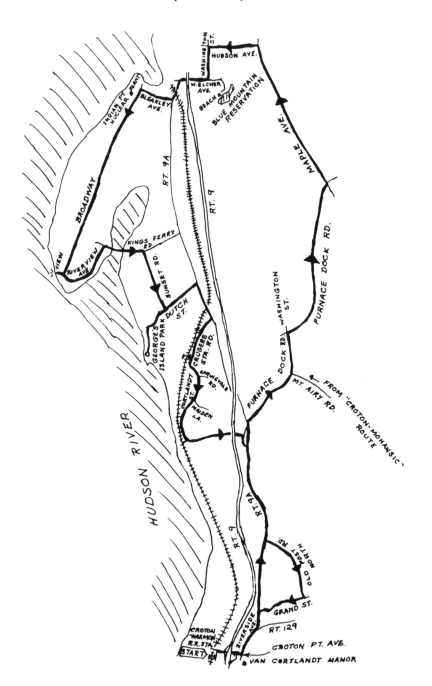

CROTON TO THE POINT (continued)

POINT TO POINT	CUME	TURN	STREET/LANDMARK
0.0	0.0	R	From the top of the hill at the exit from the Croton-Harmon railroad station parking lot, turn **right** onto **Croton Point Ave.**
0.2	0.2	L	**S. Riverside Ave.** (T; no sign)
3.3	3.5	R	**Furnace Dock Rd.**
0.8	4.3	L	To continue on **Furnace Dock Rd.** (Mt. Airy Rd. goes right)

Joint Croton route comes in here; for riders coming from the Croton-Mohansic Route, the numbers in parentheses represent your cumulative mileage

0.3	4.6	R	*(34.3)* At stop sign, to continue on **Furnace Dock Rd.** Washington St. goes straight. Do not cross steel deck bridge.
2.5	7.1	L	*(36.8)* **Maple Ave.** (stop sign)
2.5	9.6	L	*(39.3)* **Hudson Ave.** (turn is after Dean Ferris Florist, on right)
0.8	10.4	L	*(40.1)* **Washington St.**
1.0	11.4	R	*(41.1)* **Welcher Ave.** (stop sign; Ferony's Market is in front of you at this intersection). If you wish to go into **Blue Mountain Reservation,** turn **left** here instead. Bear right past the entrance station to go to the **beach**
0.3	11.7	L	*(41.4)* **Rt. 9A** (traffic light after Rt. 9 underpass; sign for Indian Point)
0.4	12.1	R	*(41.8)* **Bleakley Ave.** (toward Indian Point)
0.4	12.5	L	*(42.2)* **Broadway** (traffic light). Go **straight** here for the **energy exhibit** at Indian Point
1.7	14.2	R	*(43.9)* **Riverview Ave.** (T; no sign)
0.1	14.3		*(44.0)* Enjoy the view by the end of **Riverview Ave.,** then ride back the way you came. Go straight on Riverview Ave. (do not turn left on Broadway)
0.6	14.9	R	*(44.6)* **Kings Ferry Rd.** (T)
0.5	15.4	R	*(45.1)* **Sunset Rd.**
0.9	16.3	R	*(46.0)* **Dutch St.** (T). Enter **Georges Island Park**
0.6	16.9		*(46.6)* U-turn by boat ram in park and ride back the way you came (picnic tables available by river)
0.6	17.5	S	*(47.2)* **Dutch St.** (stop sign; Sunset Rd. goes left)
0.6	18.1	R	*(47.8)* **Rt. 9A** (T)
0.6	18.7	R	*(48.4)* **Crugers Station Rd.** (name changes to **Cortlandt St.**)

continued

CROTON TO THE POINT (continued)

POINT TO POINT	CUME	TURN	STREET/LANDMARK
0.7	19.4	**BR**	(*49.1*) At fork to continue on **Cortlandt St.** (Springvale Rd. goes left)
0.3	19.7	**BR**	(*49.4*) At fork (no sign). Cross a stream immediately
0.4	20.1	**L**	(*49.8*) At T (no sign; tracks and river close at hand on your right)
0.8	20.9	**R**	(*50.6*) **Old Albany Post Rd.** (T)
0.0	20.9	**R**	(*50.6*) **Rt. 9A** (stop sign)
1.4	22.3	**L**	(*52.0*) **Old Post Rd. North**
0.9	23.2	**R**	(*52.9*) **Grand St.** (no street sign; turn is just past St. Augustine's Church, which is on your right)
0.5	23.7	**L**	(*53.4*) **Riverside Ave.** (T)
0.8	24.5	**R**	(*54.2*) **Croton Point Ave.** (toward railroad station). Go straight if you wish to visit **Van Cortlandt Manor**
0.2	24.7	**L**	(*54.4*) Into **Croton-Harmon railroad station parking lot** (end of route)

PEEKSKILL HOLLOW RIDE   35.6 miles

Terrain: Gently rolling in the "hollows" with some larger climbs in between.
Traffic: Light to none, except moderate near Peekskill and on Rt. 301.
Road Conditions: Good. One small section of unpaved road (Horton Brook Rd.).
Points of Interest: Cycling lightly travelled "hollows" in backwoods Putnam County; **Clarence Fahnestock Park** (beach, picnic area); **Sprout Brook Park** (beach, **water slide**).

Despite the growth of New York's outer suburbs, much of Putnam County remains quiet and lightly populated. This is partly because of geography—southwestern Putnam is a land of deep stream valleys (hollows) and few roads. This route travels long distances alongside Peekskill Hollow and Canopus creeks, enabling you to enjoy this intimate countryside with few big climbs.

Start on the edge of Peekskill and head to Putnam Valley, a growing settlement on the Westchester-Putnam county line. The turn onto Peekskill Hollow Rd., will be your last direction change for 12 miles. Every four miles or so you'll pass a tiny crossroads settlement with a gas station and general store. In between there are woods, small homes and farms and views of the hills that rise steeply out of the hollow.

Ride up Rt. 301 into the heart of Clarence Fahnestock State Park. A fine beach on Canopus Lake will cool you off, and shady picnic groves are also available.

Return to Peekskill by following Canopus Creek. This is a very remote area where many of the roads were only recently paved and still very lightly travelled. Near the end of the route you will pass Sprout Brook Park, which has the area's only water slide, and a very nice lake beach.

Directions to Starting Point: Hampton Oaks IGA Supermarket Shopping Center is located on North Division St. in Peekskill. Take either Rt. 9 or the Taconic Pkwy. to the Bear Mountain Pkwy., exit at Division St. and turn left. The shopping center will be on the right in less than half a mile.
Metro-North Directions: (2 miles each way from station to start of ride). Take a Hudson Line train to Peekskill (you may have to change trains at Croton-Harmon). Turn left (north) after detraining, then make the first right onto Hudson Ave. Go under Rt. 9, then make the first left onto unmarked South St. (toward Jan Peek Square). At the T, go left onto South Division St. Bear right at the monument to continue on North Division St. and on up to the starting point. Cyclists should note that the route from the Peekskill station does not go through the nicest of neighborhoods, and might wish to be back at the station before dark.

PEEKSKILL HOLLOW RIDE (continued)

POINT TO POINT	CUME	TURN	STREET/LANDMARK
0.0	0.0	R	Exit parking lot of Hampton Oaks IGA Supermarket Shopping Center and turn **right** onto **N. Division St.** Road changes name to **Oregon Rd.**
2.1	2.1	BL	At traffic light, to continue on **Oregon Rd.** Red Mill Rd. and Westbrook Rd. go right
0.7	2.8	L	At traffic light (no signs; Old Oregon Medical Center is on the right)
0.1	2.9	R	At traffic light onto **Peekskill Hollow Rd.** (no sign) toward Adams Corners, Tompkins Corners and Taconic Pkwy.
2.5	5.4	S	At traffic light. Adams Corner **deli** on the left
4.0	9.4		Tompkins Corner **store** on the left
1.1	10.5	S	Go under Taconic State Pkwy.
4.0	14.5	L	**Rt. 301** (T). **Deli** on the left immediately after the turn
5.3	19.8	S	Go over Taconic State Pkwy.
0.3	20.1		Turn **right** for **Canopus Lake Beach Area**
3.3	23.4	L	Turn before "hill" sign toward **Taconic Outdoor Education Center**
0.7	24.1	R	At T
1.9	26.0	S	S. Highland Rd. goes right. You are now on **Dennytown Rd.**
1.3	27.3	S	Name changes to **Canopus Hollow Rd.** Canopus Hill Rd. goes right
0.5	27.8	R	**Horton Hollow Rd.** (no sign). Turn is just past a white house, onto a dirt road which crosses a small bridge
0.9	28.7	R	**County Rt. 15** (T; paved road; no sign)
2.4	31.1	BL	**Continental Village Rd. Store** on right after turn
0.6	31.7	R	**Sprout Brook Rd.**
1.7	33.4		**Sprout Brook Park** and **water slide** on left
0.6	34.0	L	**Albany Post Rd.** (T). Road changes name to **Highland Ave.**
0.7	34.7	L	**Garfield Ave.**
0.1	34.8	R	**Harrison Ave.**
0.1	34.9	L	**Warren Ave.**
0.1	35.0	L	**Division St.** (T; no sign)
0.6	35.6	R	Into parking area of **Hampton Oaks IGA Supermarket Shopping Center**

PEEKSKILL HOLLOW RIDE
(35.6 miles)

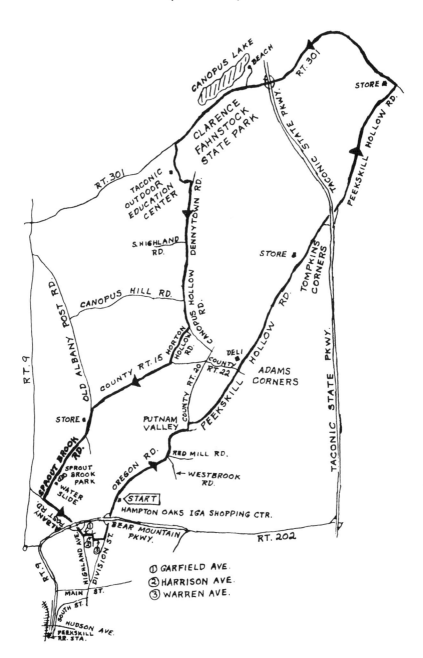

RIDES STARTING IN

BERGEN AND ROCKLAND COUNTIES

West of the Hudson the land rises more abruptly than it does on the Westchester side. Prominent hills and mountains, rare in Westchester, dot the landscape of Rockland County. And Bergen County has the Palisades, that huge riverside cliff that forces the cyclist to ride uphill instead of down to reach the Hudson.

Suburbia and overcrowded roads have overrun most of Bergen and much of Rockland. But thanks to the Palisades Interstate Park Commission, there is still a lot of great riding in this section, featuring woods, hills, views—and lots of history, because the Hudson Valley was a major theater of the Revolutionary War.

Fort Lee-Nyack heads up the Palisades. Weekend cyclists out before noon can enjoy exclusive use of a road below the cliffs with incredible views of all of metropolitan New York across the river. Piermont has a pier that reaches a mile into the river, and Nyack is well-known for antiques and good restaurants. You can head back from Nyack immediately, passing Tappan and another Washington's Headquarters enroute, or combine with the Nyack Ride.

The **Nyack Ride** is an easy loop which features a 2.5-mile bike path along the river under Hook Mountain and only one terrible hill—rising up the side of this mountain from river level to Rockland Lake State Park. This loop also passes Tappan and the Piermont Pier, and includes a side trip to a quiet swimming pool in Tallman Mountain State Park.

Saddle River-Stony Point passes rural and woodsy stretches of Bergen and Rockland en route to Stony Point. This hilly peninsula on the Hudson was the site of a successful sneak attack on the British by General "Mad Anthony" Wayne. You will not go thirsty or hungry negotiating the many climbs of this ride—the route passes a winery and innumerable country stores and delicatessens.

Two challenging routes start at Bear Mountain Inn—but a good part of the challenge is selecting which of the many points of interest you should spend time at. **Bear Mountain-Harriman** features the hills of Harriman State Park and is particularly beautiful in the fall. A steady climb of over 1,000 feet can be rewarded by a swim in Lake Welsh. Count the lakes on Seven Lakes Drive—the largest, Tiorati, could be in Minnesota with its many islands and channels between them. Another climb up Long Mountain is followed by a 10-mile descent into West Point.

There are so many things to see along **Both Sides of the Hudson** that you could spend three days doing this route. Among the highlights are West Point, Storm King Arts Center, New Windsor Cantonment, Washington's Head-quarters in Newburgh, Cold Spring shops, Boscobel restoration and Garrison art galleries. On top of all this are the most breathtaking views of the finest river valley in America—from the West Point parade grounds, along Storm King Highway, on the Newburgh-Beacon Bridge bike path, under Breakneck Ridge, at the Bear Mountain Bridge and countless places in between.

FORT LEE-NYACK   **40.8 miles**

Terrain: Hilly in spots, especially long, extended hills near the Palisades, but long stretches (such as Rt. 9W in New Jersey) are fairly flat.
Traffic: Heavy in Englewood, otherwise light to moderate. Henry Hudson Drive is traffic-free during bike hours.
Road Conditions: Good. No dirt, not even on the bike paths.
Points of Interest: Fort Lee Historic Park (visitor's center; interpretive trails and great views of Manhattan); views from the **Palisades** and **Tallman Mountain;** uncrowded swimming pool at **Tallman Mountain State Park; Nyack** shops and restaurants; **Washington's Headquarters** and town green in **Tappan; George Washington Bridge** walkway.

Henry **Hudson** Drive is an old scenic road which provides dramatic views of the metropolis across the river while you cycle through the near wilderness of Palisades Interstate Park. We recommend you start this route before 9 a.m. on a Saturday or Sunday so you can take advantage of the drive. This road is only open to bicycles before noon on weekends (April 15-November 1).

Rt. 9W is a major thoroughfare for cyclists headed north out of New York City (most of the cars are on the nearby Palisades Pkwy., leaving 9W relatively car-free north of Englewood). Divert off 9W in New York State to ride into Tallman Mountain State Park. There's a nice pool where you can cool off in season for just 50 cents.

Head up toward the wide Tappan Zee through the appropriately named village of Grand View (for an even better view of the bridge, take a side trip to the Piermont Pier). In Nyack, check out the shops but we recommend waiting for lunch until you reach Tappan because you must cross the hills of Blauvelt State Park after Nyack.

Tappan has a green, some old buildings to explore and a Washington's Headquarters museum. The return route is inland through wealthy Bergen County suburbs. East Clinton Ave. is a very long up, up, up to the top of the Palisades—then it's flat or downhill back to Fort Lee. Be sure to take a spin out onto the George Washington Bridge pedestrian path at the end of the route.

FORT LEE-NYACK (continued)

Directions to Starting Point: Fort Lee Historic park is located just south of the George Washington Bridge. If you are driving across the bridge, take the first Fort Lee exit, then keep turning left until you reach Hudson Terrace, the last street before the river. Turn right, and the park entrance is a left turn. From New Jersey, use the second Fort Lee exit (immediately before the bridge toll booths). Turn left to Hudson Terrace, then right to the park, which is on the left. Cyclists from New York City may ride across the bridge from 178th Street, then turn left at the end of the walkway and go 0.1 miles to the park, on the left.

Note: This route may be combined with the Nyack Ride for a 53.4-mile route. At Mile 18.5, in Nyack, turn right onto Main Street, then left onto Gedney Street, which is the beginning of the Nyack Ride. At Mile 19.8 of the Nyack Ride, rejoin the Fort Lee-Nyack route at Mile 25.8.

POINT TO POINT	CUME	TURN	STREET/LANDMARK
0.0	0.0		Ride down exit road of Fort Lee Historic Park from the Visitor's Center
0.1	0.1	R	**Hudson Terrace** (T)
2.1	2.2	L	**Palisade Ave.** (T)
			If you are at this point before noon on a weekend, turn **right** and proceed down toward **Englewood Boat Basin**. Fork **left** onto **Henry Hudson Dr.**, which you follow for 5 miles. Near the Alpine Boat Basin, climb back up toward Rt. 9W, then turn **right** on Rt. 9W to resume the route about 4 miles south of the New York State border
0.1	2.3	R	**Sylvan Ave./Rt. 9W** (traffic light)
9.1	11.4		Entering New York State
1.1	12.5	R	Onto **bike path** (just past "Indian Motorcycle" sign on right)
1.3	13.8	R	At end of bike path (T)
0.2	14.0	R	At T; follow **bike route** signs
0.1	14.1	R	At traffic circle toward **pool** (following bike route signs)
0.1	14.2	L	To continue on **bike path**. Turn **sharp right** to go to Tallman Mountain **pool**

continued

FORT LEE-NYACK (continued)

POINT TO POINT	CUME	TURN	STREET/LANDMARK
0.5	14.7	**R**	At end of path. Cross steel deck bridge onto **Piermont Ave.**
0.1	14.8		Turn **right** onto **Paradise Ave.** for side trip to Piermont Pier
3.7	18.5	**L**	**Main St.,** downtown Nyack (T). *Turn right here to join Nyack ride. Go to Gedney St. and turn left.*
0.7	19.2	**L**	**Rt. 9W** (traffic light at crest of hill)
0.1	19.3	**BR**	After crossing Thruway onto **S. Highland Ave.** (sign for Nyack College)
0.3	19.6	**S**	Street name changes to **South Boulevard**
0.9	20.5	**S**	At unmarked intersection. Street name changes to **Clausland Mtn. Rd.**
2.5	23.0	**L**	**Greenbush Rd. South**
0.7	23.7	**R**	Toward **Rt. 303**
0.0	23.7	**L**	**Rt. 303 South** (traffic light)
0.3	24.0	**R**	**Orangeburg Rd.** (traffic light)
0.2	24.2	**L**	**Western Highway** (first traffic light)
1.2	25.4	**L**	**Greenbush Rd.** (street sign is hidden on the left. You will cross over railroad tracks shortly after the turn)
0.4	25.8	**S**	At stop sign onto **Kings Highway.** The small Tappan town green is on your right (*Riders from the Nyack Ride, rejoin here*)
0.1	25.9	**S**	At the traffic light, crossing Old Tappan Rd.
0.1	26.0	**L**	**Oak Tree Rd.**
0.2	26.2		**George Washington's Headquarters museum** on right
0.2	26.4	**S**	Cross Rt. 303
0.9	27.3	**R**	**Rt. 340**
0.4	27.7		Name changes to **Piermont Rd.** at New Jersey border
3.5	31.2	**S**	Cross Closter Dock Rd.
0.8	32.0	**L**	Curve **left** onto **County Rd./Rt. 501 South. Deli** on right shortly before the turn
0.6	32.6	**R**	Curve **right** to continue on **Rt. 501 South** (Anderson Rd. goes left)

continued

FORT LEE-NYACK (continued)

POINT TO POINT	CUME	TURN	STREET/LANDMARK
1.0	33.6		Historic **Captain John Huyler** house on left
1.0	34.6	L	At traffic light to continue on **Rt. 501 South**
0.1	34.7	S	At blinking red light onto **E. Clinton Ave./County Rt. 72** (Dean Dr. goes right)
2.0	36.7	R	**Rt. 9W South** (T)
1.8	38.5	L	**Palisade Ave.** (traffic light)
0.1	38.6	R	**Hudson Terrace**
2.1	40.7	L	Into **Fort Lee Historic Park**
0.1	40.8		**Visitor's Center** (end of route)

FORT LEE-NYACK
(40.8 miles)

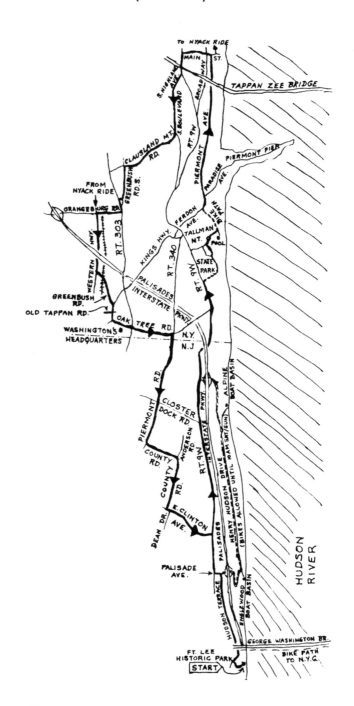

NYACK RIDE
(26.3 miles)

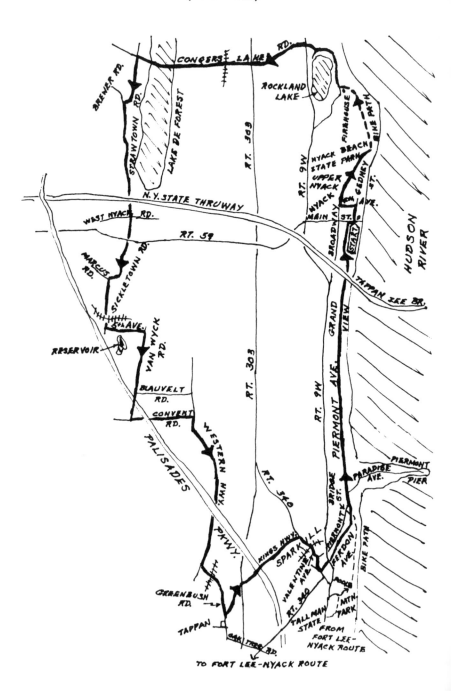

NYACK RIDE   26.3 miles

Terrain: Mostly rolling hills inland and flat along the Hudson River. There is one killer ascent from the river to Rockland Lake State Park.

Traffic: Light to moderate, except heavier near Congers and West Nyack. No traffic at all along the Hudson River bike path north of Nyack!

Road Conditions: Pretty good, with occasional bumpy spots. The 2½ mile bike path is unpaved, but very smooth and rock-free. Many roads have no shoulders.

Points of Interest: Nyack shops and restaurants; Hudson River bike path in **Nyack State Park; Rockland Lake State Park** (swimming and boating); historic **Tappan;** the **Piermont Pier;** swimming at **Tallman Mountain State Park.**

Nyack is a scenic and interesting Hudson River town and the perfect place to begin and end this fairly easy tour of southeastern Rockland County. Its antique shops and good eateries attract large crowds every weekend.

The route gets you away from the crowds quickly, heading north along Broadway into posh Upper Nyack. Beautiful homes grace this broad boulevard, and little traffic bothers cyclists. The reason for the light traffic looms ahead in the form of Hook Mountain: Cars must turn around at Nyack State Park while bikes may continue under the mountain along the river, with fine views south to the Tappan Zee and across to Sing Sing Prison.

You may wish to walk the long, very steep hill up from the river. A quick dip in the pool at Rockland Lake State Park might be in order on a hot day, but we recommend swimming at the smaller, much less crowded pool at Tallman Mountain State Park near the end of the ride.

Cycling inland, you pass Congers, where food is available. Next, descend to and cross Lake DeForest. The route then heads south to historic Tappan, where an exploring cyclist can find several historic houses and a pleasant town green.

In a couple of miles you are back on the Hudson. A bike path leads to the aforementioned pool at Tallman Mountain, where admission is only 50 cents. Riders may wish to take an additional detour to the Piermont Pier. An unpaved road leads onto the pier, formerly a railroad-ferry terminal, now a parklike peninsula that sticks a full mile into the river.   The final part of the route passes more fine homes in the appropriately named village of Grand View before returning to Nyack.

NYACK RIDE (continued)

Directions to Starting Point: The route begins at the intersection of **Gedney and Main St.** in downtown Nyack, which is the last turn off Main St. before it reaches the Hudson River. If you are driving from the Tappan Zee Bridge, use Exit 11 off the New York Thruway. Go straight at the end of the ramp, proceed to the second light (Midland Ave.) and turn right. Main St. is the first light; turn left. From the southbound New York Thruway, take Exit 11 and turn left at the end of the ramp. This is Route 59, which leads you directly onto Main St. after you cross Route 9W. Parking is available on the street and in nearby municipal lots.

Note: You may easily combine this ride with the Ft. Lee-Nyack Route (p. 87) for a 53.4-mile trek. See the Ft. Lee-Nyack write-up and cue sheet for directions.

POINT TO POINT	CUME	TURN	STREET/LANDMARK
0.0	0.0		Start ride at intersection of **Gedney St.** and **Main St.** Ride north on **Gedney St.** (The Hudson River will be on your right).
0.2	0.2	L	**4th Avenue**
0.2	0.4	R	**North Broadway** (stop sign; no street sign)
1.7	2.1	R	Into **Nyack State Park.** Go down the hill. (Restrooms and water on left at bottom of hill.)
0.3	2.4	S	Onto **bike route.** Near end of bike path bear **left** at fork.
2.5	4.9		Emerge from bike path and climb large hill.
0.4	5.3	R	At fork (no sign). Fork is just past firehouse on left. **Rockland Lake State Park** will be on your left.
1.0	6.3	R	Toward **Rt. 9W.**
0.1	6.4	S	Cross Rt. 9W onto **Lake Rd.**
0.3	6.7	S	Cross Rt. 303
0.5	7.2	S	Through Congers where there are two delicatessens
0.2	7.4	S	Cross Kings Highway
1.3	8.7	L	**Strawtown Road** (First turn past lake)
2.3	11.0	L	At T and stop sign to continue on **Strawtown Rd.** (Brewer Rd. goes right)
1.6	12.6	S	At stop sign to continue on **Strawtown Rd.**
0.7	13.3	S	Cross W. Nyack Rd. at light onto **Sickletown Rd.**
1.0	14.3	L	To continue on **Sickletown Rd.** (Marcus Rd. goes right)

continued

NYACK RIDE (continued)

POINT TO POINT	CUME	TURN	STREET/LANDMARK
0.8	15.1	L	**5th Avenue** (immediately after tunnel)
0.5	15.6	R	**Van Wyck Rd.** (T)
0.9	16.5	L	**Convent Rd.** (T)
0.9	17.4	R	**Western Highway South** (T)
2.0	19.4	BL	**Greenbush Rd.** (Street sign is hidden on the left. You will go over a railroad crossing shortly after the turn)
0.4	19.8	SL	**Kings Highway** (stop sign). **Bear right** to go into **Tappan** (town green; old houses) *Riders going to Fort Lee: Continue at Mile 25.8 of Fort Lee-Nyack ride).*
0.6	20.4	S	Cross Rt. 303
0.9	21.3	BR	**Rt. 340** (yield sign)
0.2	21.5	S	Cross railroad tracks at traffic light
0.1	21.6	R	**Valentine Avenue**
0.0	21.6	BL	Continue on **Rt. 340**
0.1	21.7	L	**Ferdon Ave.** (toward Piermont).
0.8	22.5		Turn **right** across from Bridge St. (on left) for **1**-mile bike path to **swimming pool** at Tallman Mountain State Park begins across from Bridge St. (on left)
0.0	22.5	L	Over bridge onto **Piermont Avenue.** (After crossing bridge turn **right** onto **Paradise Avenue** for side trip to nice houses and Piermont Pier).
3.7	26.2	R	**Main St.** (T)
0.1	26.3		Intersection of **Main** and **Gedney Sts.** and end of ride.

SADDLE RIVER-STONY POINT
(45.9 miles)

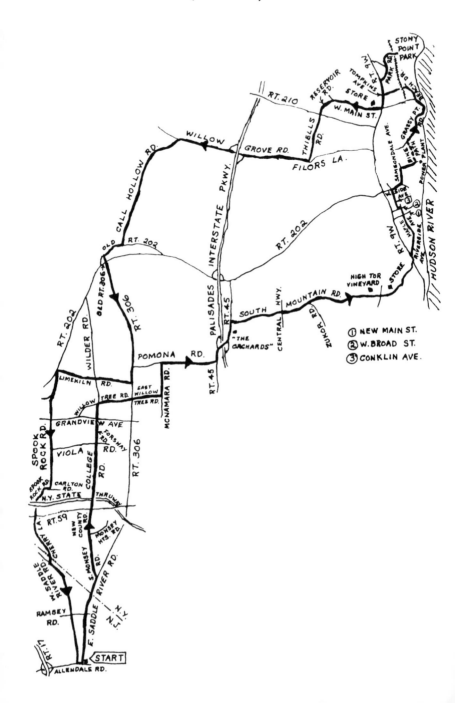

① NEW MAIN ST.
② W. BROAD ST.
③ CONKLIN AVE.

SADDLE RIVER-STONY POINT   45.9 miles

Terrain: Easy going in New Jersey and near Grassy Point. Otherwise, rolling to downright hilly.
Traffic: Mostly light, with a few brief moderate sections.
Road Conditions: Mostly good, but some rough pavement, especially on South Mountain Rd.
Points of Interest: High Tor Winery and Vineyards; Stony Point State Historic Park, picnic areas, visitor's center, historic lighthouse; views of hills and Hudson.

Most people think of Storm King, Crow's Nest and the other mountains near West Point when they think of the Hudson Highlands. The southern extremity of that range of hills is in northern Rockland County, and this route gives you great views of the higher hills while riding over the ''lower'' hills.

Start in Saddle River, a still-rural (in appearance) part of Bergen County. Head north on the back roads of Monsey and Pomona in Rockland County. The hills of Harriman Park rise in the distance, and are especially spectacular in the fall.

South Mountain Road is an old, windy, bumpy road that takes you under High Tor to Haverstraw. The road starts in a working orchard and passes a vineyard. After you pass a quarry, slow down as you enter a cut in the rock—the busy intersection of Rt. 9W comes up suddenly, as the view of Haverstraw unfolds.

Next, go through Haverstraw, a quiet old industrial town which provides a change of pace from the fields and woodlands earlier in the ride. The riverfront area of Grassy Point contains a huge factory, but also has several marinas and some interesting small homes and bars right on the river.

Stony Point is a rocky promontory that juts into the Hudson River opposite Verplanck. It is here that General ''Mad Anthony'' Wayne crept up on the British in 1779 and boosted the Colonial Army's morale with his surprise victory. Today there are fine picnic areas overlooking the river, an old lighthouse and lots of wild raspberries to look forward to in July.

The return route takes you through two of the more remote back roads of Rockland (Call Hollow and Spook Rock) before coming back to Saddle River.
Directions to Starting Point: This route starts at the intersection of **Allendale Rd.** and **E. Saddle River Rd.** in Saddle River. Use the Saddle River/ Woodcliff Lake exit off Rt. 17 and proceed ¾ mile. Parking is available in several lots nearby, including the Colonial Park Shopping Center just up E. Saddle River Rd. from the intersection.

SADDLE RIVER-STONY POINT (continued)

POINT TO POINT	CUME	TURN	STREET/LANDMARK
0.0	0.0		From the intersection of Allendale Rd. and E. Saddle River Rd. (County Rt. 75), proceed north on **E. Saddle River Rd.** (the Texaco Station and the post office will be on your left)
3.4	3.4		Enter New York State
0.8	4.2	L	**S. Monsey Rd.**
1.2	5.4	S	Name changes to **New County Rd.** (Monsey Heights Rd. goes right)
0.7	6.1	S	Cross Rt. 59. Road changes name to **College Rd.**
1.9	8.0	S	Cross Viola Rd. Road changes name to **Forshay Rd.**
1.3	9.3	R	**Willow Tree Rd.** (street sign is on the left)
0.8	10.1	S	Cross Rt. 306. Road changes name to **E. Willow Tree Rd.**
0.9	11.0	L	**McNamara Rd.** (T)
0.7	11.7	R	**Pomona Rd.** (T)
1.2	12.9	L	**Rt. 45** (T)
0.7	13.6	R	**South Mountain Rd.** (just past ''The Orchards'' fruit market)
1.7	15.3	S	At blinking light, to continue on **South Mountain Rd.**
0.7	16.0	BL	To continue on **South Mountain Rd.** (Zukor Rd. goes right)
1.6	17.6		**High Tor Vineyards and Winery** on left
0.1	17.7	S	At stop sign (no street sign) to continue on **South Mountain Rd. Store** on left after intersection
0.8	18.5	BL	**Rt. 9W.** CAUTION: Slow down as you enter rock cut going downhill: the traffic light at the bottom comes up suddenly!
0.1	18.6	R	At first right, by Tilcon Plant sign, onto **Riverside Ave.** (no street sign)
1.1	19.7	S	Cross New Main St. Road has changed name to **Maple Ave.**
0.1	19.8	L	**W. Broad St.**
0.1	19.9	R	**Conklin Ave.**
0.3	20.2	R	**West Side Ave.** (traffic light)
0.1	20.3	L	**Samsondale Ave.**
0.2	20.5	R	Toward power plant and **W. Haverstraw Recreation Area**

continued

SADDLE RIVER-STONY POINT (continued)

POINT TO POINT	CUME	TURN	STREET/LANDMARK
0.1	20.6	BL	Onto **bike route** by power plant
0.3	20.9	S	At end of bike path onto **Beach Rd.** (no sign). Becomes **Grassy Point Rd.** (no signs)
2.0	22.9	R	**Beach Dr.**
0.5	23.4	L	At stop sign under very low railroad underpass onto **Tompkins Ave.** (no sign). Road goes uphill
0.6	24.0	R	**Rt. 9W/202** (T; yield sign)
0.3	24.3	R	**Park Rd.**
0.3	24.6	S	Toward **Stony Point Park** (bike route signs point left here)
0.4	25.0		Leave bike at rack and climb up hill to picnic area and lighthouse. Ride back the way you came after visiting the park
0.4	25.4	S	At yield sign, returning the way you came
0.2	25.6	L	**Rt. 9W** (T)
0.7	26.3	R	**W. Main St.** (traffic light). **Store** on right after turn
0.8	27.1	BL	**Reservoir Rd.**
0.3	27.4	S	Cross Rt. 210 at stop sign onto **Thiells Rd.**
0.8	28.2	R	**Filors Lane** (T). Road will change name to **Willow Grove Rd.**
1.3	29.5	S	Ride under Palisades Pkwy.
0.5	30.0	L	**Call Hollow Rd.**
2.9	32.9	R	**Old Rt. 202** (T)
0.3	33.2	L	**Old Rt. 306**
0.1	33.3	S	Cross Rt. 202 at traffic light onto **Rt. 306**
1.5	34.8	R	**Lime Kiln Rd.** (traffic light)
1.3	36.1	SL	**Spook Rock Rd.** (T). CAUTION: Steep hill before this intersection—control speed. Do not turn onto Rt. 202
0.7	36.8	BL	At fork to continue on **Spook Rock Rd.** (Old Rt. 202 goes right)
0.4	37.2	S	Cross Grandview Ave. at stop sign
2.1	39.3	R	At T to continue on **Spook Rock Rd.** (Carlton Rd. goes left)
0.5	39.8	S	Go under N.Y. Thruway
0.2	40.0	S	Cross Rt. 59 at traffic light. Road changes name to **Cherry Lane**
2.0	42.0	L	**W. Saddle River Rd.** (T)
3.8	45.8	L	**E. Allendale Rd.** (traffic light)
0.1	45.9		Intersection of **Allendale Rd.** and **E. Saddle River Rd.** (end of route)

BEAR MOUNTAIN-HARRIMAN
(41.4 miles)

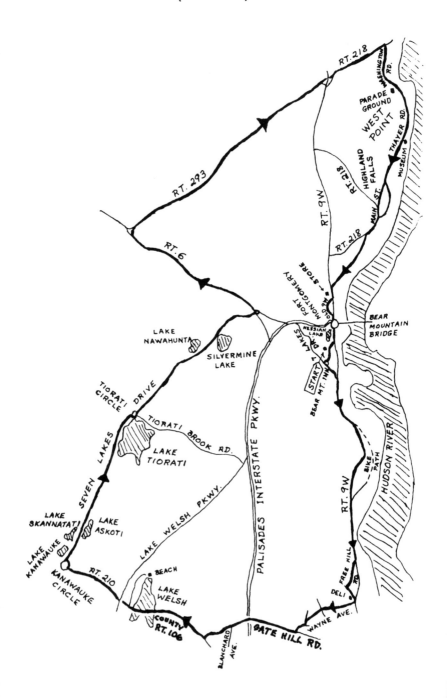

BEAR MOUNTAIN-HARRIMAN   41.4 miles

Terrain: This is one of the hilliest rides in the book, yet any cyclist who rides regularly will have no trouble. The hills are long and well-graded, for the most part.

Traffic: Totally dependent on the season. Harriman Park roads are quiet most weekdays and non-summer weekends, but can be extremely busy on summer weekends. Off-season, Seven Lakes Drive is as empty as a backwoods hiking trail. Long Mountain Pkwy. and Rt. 9W, however, are always busy.

Road Conditions: Excellent.

Points of Interest: Bear Mountain Park (hiking, zoo and museum); **Lake Welsh** (swimming); **West Point.**

Bear Mountain and Harriman State Parks contain 54,000 acres of mountains, woods, lakes and streams. While this area is quite popular on summer weekends, at other times cyclists could easily imagine themselves very deep in the wilderness rather than a short 40 miles from Times Square. Fall is an especially great time for this route because there are so many tree-covered mountains turning colors.

Start at Bear Mountain Inn. Descend to river level, then either climb the shoulder of Dunderberg Mountain with the highway or use the unpaved (and officially closed) bike path. The bike path is a better alternative because it provides spectacular views of the marshes near Iona Island.

Turn west at Tompkins Cove and ride on Wayne Avenue, a pleasant woodsy road named for General ''Mad Anthony'' Wayne. When you reach Rt. 210, prepare for a long, steady, seemingly endless climb to Lake Welsh (elevation 1,015 feet). A swim feels so good right now!

A wild, fast, curvy roller-coaster downhill takes you to Kanawauke Circle and onto Seven Lakes Drive. The view of Lake Tiorati with its islands is particularly breathtaking. After passing Tiorati Circle, it's a straight, fast, almost four-mile downhill to the big, busy traffic circle where you will begin a three-mile climb up Long Mountain. Busy Rt. 6 has a wide shoulder for this climb.

The work is worth it because you then enjoy ten miles of almost continuous downhill or flat terrain into West Point. Traffic is light and there are superb views of undeveloped mountainous land owned by the Military Academy. West Point contains the finest vantage points for river and mountain scenery in the Hudson Valley. Return to Bear Mountain via the homey villages of Highland Falls and Fort Montgomery.

BEAR MOUNTAIN-HARRIMAN (continued)

Directions to Starting Point: Bear Mountain Inn is at the northern end of the Palisades Pkwy. and the western end of the Bear Mountain Bridge. Head south on Rt. 9W from the traffic circle where these roads meet. Bear right at the traffic light in 0.4 miles, then turn right into the Inn. There is a parking fee.

Metro-North Directions: (6.3 miles each way from the station). Take a Hudson Line train to Garrison (you will probably have to change trains at Croton-Harmon). Turn right after detraining, and head up the hill to Rt. 9D. Go south on Rt. 9D to the Bear Mountain Bridge. Cross the bridge, go south on Rt. 9W, then bear right at the traffic light to the Bear Mountain Inn.

POINT TO POINT	CUME	TURN	STREET/LANDMARK
0.0	0.0		Start at the south end of the Bear Mountain Inn parking lot. Exit toward **Rt. 9W South**
0.2	0.2	L	Go two-thirds of the way around Bear Mt. Circle toward **Rts. 9W/202 South**
0.7	0.9	BR	**Rt. 9W/202 South** (T) In about 0.3 miles, choose between riding over the mountain on **Rt. 9W** or bearing left to ride on the (unpaved but smooth) old road, the officially closed bike route which will rejoin Rt. 9W in about 2.5 miles.
5.2	6.1	R	**Free Hill Rd.** (by Lynch's Restaurant)
0.3	6.4	L	At T and stop sign (no street sign)
0.2	6.6	BR	**Rt. 9W/202 South** (T). **Deli** on the right at the intersection
0.0	6.6	R	**Wayne Ave.**
0.8	7.4	S	To continue on **Wayne Ave.** (no street sign)
0.6	8.0	R	At stop sign (no street sign)
0.2	8.2	R	**Gate Hill Rd.** (T)
2.9	11.1	BR	No sign (**Harriman State Park** sign on right shortly after turn) (road becomes **County Route 106** at Orange County Line)
1.9	13.0		Turn **right** to go to Lake Welsh beach
1.7	14.7	SR	At Kanawauke Circle onto **Seven Lakes Drive** toward Lake Tiorati
3.3	18.0		Go halfway around Tiorati Circle to continue on **Seven Lakes Drive**
3.8	21.8		Go seven-eighths the way around traffic circle onto **Rt. 6 West**
3.3	25.1	SR	**Rt. 293**

continued

BEAR MOUNTAIN-HARRIMAN (continued)

POINT TO POINT	CUME	TURN	STREET/LANDMARK
6.8	31.9	**L**	**Rt. 218**
0.1	32.0	**BL**	To continue on **Rt. 218 North**
1.2	33.2	**R**	Enter **West Point** at Washington Gate. Follow **Washington Rd.** and **Thayer Rd.** past Parade Ground
3.2	36.4		Exit West Point at **Thayer Gate** Go **left** to bypass Highland Falls or **right** to pedal through town
0.7	37.1	**S**	Both roads meet at. fountain. Continue on **Main St./Rt. 218 South**
0.7	37.8	**BL**	Near "Speed Limit 40" sign toward Grace Baptist Church (turn is before Academy Motel)
1.3	39.1	**L**	**Rt. 9W**
0.8	39.9	**BR**	**Old Rt. 9W** (no sign; by Sunoco station; **store** on right after turn)
0.5	40.4	**BR**	**Rt. 9W**
0.5	40.9		Go halfway around the circle to continue on **Rt. 9W South**
0.4	41.3	**BR**	At traffic light
0.1	41.4	**R**	Into **Bear Mountain Inn** (end of route)

BOTH SIDES OF THE HUDSON
(48.9 miles)

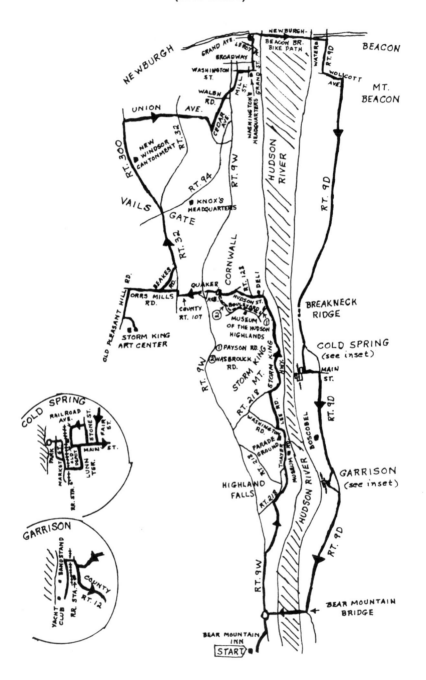

BOTH SIDES OF THE HUDSON   48.9 miles

Terrain: Some hills going up and down from the river, but mostly very gentle rollers.

Traffic: Mostly moderate, because there are few side roads in this area.

Road Conditions: Good, except Rt. 9D in Beacon which is perenially under construction.

Points of Interest: West Point (military museum, parade ground, chapels, and views); **Storm King Highway; Museum of the Hudson Highlands; Cornwall-on-Hudson** and **Cornwall; Storm King Art Center,** a huge modern sculpture garden; **New Windsor Cantonment** (state historic site, a colonial winter camp); **Washington's Headquarters** in Newburgh; riding across the 2-mile **Newburgh-Beacon Bridge; Cold Spring** (shops and riverfront park); **Boscobel Restoration; Garrison** galleries; **Bear Mountain** Bridge, Park and Inn.

The Hudson Highlands are as majestic now as when Thomas Cole and other 19th Century artists sat near the river and sketched Storm King, Crow's Nest, Bull Hill and other peaks that rise as much as 1,000 feet from river level. You will catch all the prime vistas as you cycle riverfront roads, one of which is carved into a mountainside.

Thanks to the addition of a bike path on the newer of the Newburgh-Beacon twin spans, it is now possible to make a loop trip, enabling you to enjoy different views coming and going. There are so many things to see and do—you could easily spend three days on this route!

Start at Bear Mountain, a park worthy of a day's visit in itself with its inn, zoo, boating lake and miles of fine hiking. Head through West Point. You may wish to divert off the route to visit the chapels and the stadium, but the main route passes the parade ground and the best view of the river. Note that the museum at West Point will be closed from July 4, 1988 through sometime in 1989 as it relocates to a point near the Visitor's Center near the Thayer Gate.

Next cycle the Storm King Highway. This engineering marvel was carved into the side of the mountain and reminds many people of Route 1 in California because it curves in and out of valleys high above the water. This road is quite narrow and curvy, so be listening for traffic, which generally is light. Also, if the road is closed due to rockslides, a fairly frequent event in rainy seasons, it should still be available for cycling.

You have the choice of two routes in Cornwall—the main route through town, with its nice homes and shops, or the alternate through the woods, which passes the very interesting Museum of the Hudson Highlands (regional flora and fauna).

BOTH SIDES OF THE HUDSON (continued)

Next head to the Storm King Art Center, a major outdoor collection of large-sized modern sculpture with Storm King and Schunemunk mountains as backdrop. Head into Vails Gate next, where the historic-minded might wish a side trip to a large old house that served as General Knox's headquarters in the Revolution. Two other historical spots in the Newburgh area are passed by the main route: New Windsor Cantonment (the colonial army winter camp in 1782) and Washington's Headquarters.

After cycling through a rejuvenating part of the aged river city, cross the 2-mile bridge to Beacon and drink from the water fountain right on the path. Next, head south on Rt. 9D, climbing toward the base of 1,500-foot Mt. Beacon. A few miles further brings a glorious descent to river level—and awe-inspiring views of Storm King across the way. Tunnel under Breakneck Ridge and head into Cold Spring, a charming village of antique and crafts shops with a classic riverside park, complete with bandstand. Ice cream and other goodies are readily available.

A mile south of Cold Spring is Boscobel, a restored mansion with an incredible collection of 18th and 19th Century furniture. The gardens and river view, as well as the house tour, make it worth the admission price.

Finally comes Garrison, a tiny, quaint riverside hamlet with several art galleries and no stores to speak of. This is one town that time truly forgot, although those who saw the movie *Hello Dolly* might remember the scenery.

Historic markers talking about Benedict Arnold's treachery and the colonial attempts to chain the Hudson to shut off British ships abound on the final run to the Bear Mountain Bridge.

Directions to Starting Point: Bear Mountain Inn is at the northern end of the Palisades Parkway and the western end of the Bear Mountain Bridge. Head south on Rt. 9W from the traffic circle where these roads meet. Bear right at the traffic light in 0.4 miles, then turn right into the Inn. There is a parking fee.

Metro-North Directions: Take a Hudson Division train to Garrison or Cold Spring (you will probably have to change trains at Croton-Harmon). Join the route at Mile 42.5 or Mile 37.1, respectively.

BOTH SIDES OF THE HUDSON (continued)

POINT TO POINT	CUME	TURN	STREET/LANDMARK
0.0	0.0	**L**	Starting in front of the Bear Mountain Inn, exit toward **Rt. 9W North**
0.1	0.1	**BL**	At traffic light onto **Rt. 9W North**
0.4	0.5		At traffic circle, go halfway around to continue on **Rt. 9W North** toward West Point
1.8	2.3	**BR**	Toward Grace Baptist Church
1.3	3.6	**S**	At yield sign onto **Rt. 218/Main St.**
0.8	4.4	**BR**	At fork toward West Point. Rt. 218 goes left
0.6	5.0	**S**	Enter Thayer Gate of West Point. You are on **Thayer Rd.**
0.9	5.9	**S**	Road goes under building.
0.8	6.7	**S**	**Parade ground** on left. Road is now called **Washington Rd.**

continued

BOTH SIDES OF THE HUDSON (continued)

POINT TO POINT	CUME	TURN	STREET/LANDMARK
0.9	7.6	**R**	**Lee Rd.** toward Lee Gate. Even if gate is marked as closed, you can get through with a bike
0.7	8.3	**S**	Through Lee Gate (walk around gate if it is closed)
0.1	8.4	**BR**	At yield sign onto **Rt. 218** (Storm King Highway). Be wary of traffic!
3.8	12.2		Turn **left** at **Payson Rd.** for **Museum of the Hudson Highlands** and alternate route (slightly longer; one more hill): At T, turn **right** onto **Boulevard. Museum** will be on your left. Keep going in the same direction after visiting museum. **Bear right** at **Hasbrouck Rd.** which will take you to a traffic circle. Rejoin the route at Mile 13.9 Cyclists wishing to go through Cornwall, go **straight** at Payson Rd. intersection
0.2	12.4	**L**	To continue on **Rt. 218. Deli** on right just past turn
0.3	12.7	**BL**	At blinking light onto **Hudson St.** Rt. 218 goes right
0.6	13.3	**BL**	At traffic light onto **Main St.** (no sign). Street goes through downtown Cornwall
0.6	13.9	**BR**	At traffic circle onto **Quaker Ave.** which passes Grand Union (on your left)
0.4	14.3	**S**	Go under Rt. 9W. Road becomes **County Rt. 107**
0.5	14.8	**R**	**Rt. 32** (T)
0.2	15.0	**L**	After crossing bridge onto **Orrs Mills Rd./ County Rt. 20**
0.5	15.5	**L**	**Old Pleasant Hill Rd.** (toward Storm King Art Center)
0.2	15.7	**L**	Into **Storm King Art Center**
0.2	15.9		**U-turn** at building and ride back the way you came in
0.2	16.1	**R**	At end of driveway onto **Old Pleasant Hill Rd.** (no sign)
0.2	16.3	**R**	**Orrs Mills Rd.** (T) (no sign)
0.2	16.5	**BL**	At fork onto **Beakes Rd.**
0.4	16.9	**BL**	**Rt. 32** (T)

continued

BOTH SIDES OF THE HUDSON (continued)

POINT TO POINT	CUME	TURN	STREET/LANDMARK
1.2	18.1	BL	At light in Vails Gate onto **Rt. 300 North.** If you wish to visit **Knox's Headquarters,** turn **right** at this corner onto **Rt. 94.** The building is on the right in 0.8 miles at the corner of Forge Hill Rd.
1.2	19.3		**New Windsor Cantonment** (state historic site) on the right
1.0	20.3	SR	**Union Ave.**
1.6	21.9	S	At traffic light. Cross Rt. 32/Windsor Highway
0.7	22.6	L	**Cedar Ave.**
0.8	23.4	S	At stop sign. Cross Walsh Rd.
0.1	23.5	R	At the T
0.0	23.5	BL	Cross Rt. 9W then **bear left** onto **Mill St.** (no sign). Cross old bridge
0.7	24.2	R	**Washington St.**
0.4	24.6	S	At traffic light to cross Liberty St. **Washington's Headquarters** will be on your right
0.1	24.7	L	**Grand St.**
0.1	24.8	S	At traffic light. Cross Broadway
1.0	25.8	BL	**Leroy Pl.** (T)
0.2	26.0	R	At bike route sign onto **Grand Ave.** (no street sign)
0.3	26.3	L	Onto **bike route** crossing Newburgh-Beacon Bridge. **Water fountain** available on Beacon side of bridge, right on the path
2.0	28.3	R	At end of bike route onto **Rt. 9D South**
1.4	29.7	L	At traffic light to continue on **Rt. 9D South/ Wolcott Ave.**
1.1	30.8	R	To continue on **Rt. 9D**
3.9	34.7	S	Through tunnel under Breakneck Ridge
1.5	36.2	BR	**Fair St.** (no sign; Rt. 9D goes uphill, and Fair St. follows the river)
0.6	36.8	R	**Main St.,** Cold Spring (T)
0.0	36.8	R	**Stone St.** (first right)
0.1	36.9	L	**Railroad Ave.**
0.0	36.9	L	Curve **left** by the tracks—ice cream available in the old depot on the right
0.1	37.0	L	**Main St.**

continued

BOTH SIDES OF THE HUDSON (continued)

POINT TO POINT	CUME	TURN	STREET/LANDMARK
0.0	37.0	R	**Lunn Terrace** (immediate right)
0.1	37.1	R	After crossing railroad at yield sign onto **Market St.** (no sign)
0.1	37.2	L	**Main St.**
0.1	37.3		Turn around at bandstand and cycle back over tracks generally following the route you came over on
0.4	37.7	R	**Main St.** (T)
0.3	38.0	R	**Rt. 9D South/Chestnut St.** (traffic light)
1.1	39.1		**Boscobel Restoration** on right
2.6	41.7	R	Toward Garrison Art Center. Turn is just past a big stone church (on right)
0.4	42.1	L	Cross railroad
0.0	42.1	L	Onto road that parallels the river
0.2	42.3		Turn around at the end of the road, by the Garrison Yacht Club
0.2	42.5	R	Over railroad bridge
0.0	42.5	R	After crossing bridge onto **County Rt. 12.** Do not go up hill the way you came down
0.6	43.1	R	**Rt. 9D** (stop sign)
4.6	47.7	R	Cross **Bear Mountain Bridge**
0.6	48.3		Go three-quarters of the way around the traffic circle onto **Rt. 9W South**
0.5	48.8	BR	At traffic light toward **Bear Mountain Inn**
0.1	48.9	R	Into parking lot and inn (end of route)

RIDES STARTING IN

ORANGE COUNTY

Back in the 19th Century, all of the areas covered by this guide were open farmland. Now Westchester, Putnam and Rockland are heavily forested, but Orange County retains its open look. This is a special treat for the cyclist, because on top of every rise is a multi-mile panorama of corn and vegetable fields, dairy and sheep herds and pastureland, interrupted only by occasional houses, patches of woods, and rivers.

Orange County is starting to develop rapidly, but much of it remains rural. There are numerous interesting villages and points of interest to explore. Both rides leave from Monroe, which is no more than an hour's drive from anywhere in Westchester, Rockland, Bergen or New York City.

Monroe-Pine Island might be subtitled "onions and grapes." Pine Island is the center of a major onion producing area, and lovers of this particular vegetable will want to cycle here at harvest time just to inhale the strong aroma. Washingtonville is the home of Brotherhood Winery, where tours and tastes are available. In between you will pass through: Sugar Loaf, a working crafts village; Warwick, with its large Main Street homes and small meditation center; and Chester, home of antique shops and a "ghost town" Main Street.

Monroe-Montgomery heads north and west to the Wallkill Valley. Among the highlights, besides delightful rural pedaling, are a farm museum, a ski hill with a commanding view, an art gallery with excellent Hudson Valley prints, and a huge railroad trestle coming out of a mountainside.

MONROE-PINE ISLAND
(49.5 or 60.5 miles)

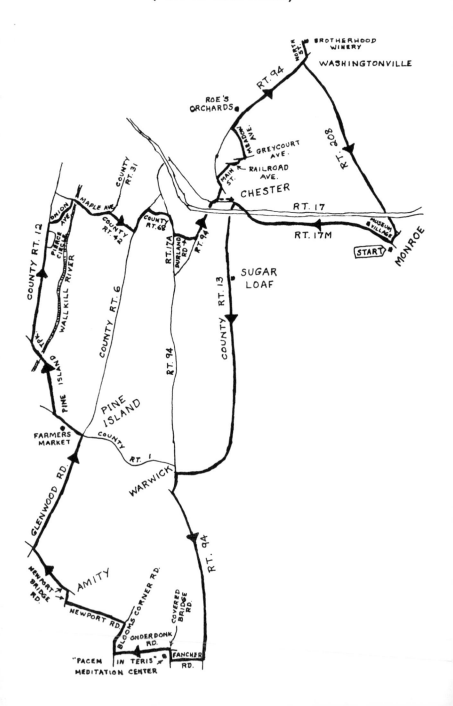

MONROE-PINE ISLAND   49.5 or 60.5 miles

Terrain: Gently rolling. Some hills, but much easier terrain than, say, northern Westchester or Rockland. Flat as a pancake near Pine Island.
Traffic: Mostly light to nonexistent, except a bit busier into and out of Warwick, Chester and Washingtonville.
Road Conditions: Generally excellent. One 0.8-mile flat stretch of dirt road.
Points of Interest: Museum Village in Monroe; craft and arts stores in **Sugar Loaf;** Pacem in Teris **meditation center** (outdoor sculpture garden by stream); **Pine Island** (onion fields and incredibly low-priced **farmers market); Chester** antique shops and "ghost town" section; Roe's Orchards **(apples); Brotherhood Winery** in Washingtonville.

Open vistas of cows and cornfields, several interesting villages and the East Coast's major onion producing area are the rewards of this long cycle tour.

The mileage may make this look like an ambitious tour but cyclists of average ability should not have any trouble because the terrain is gentle. Riders who have overestimated their ability may cut off 11 miles by returning to Monroe from Chester.

Start in Monroe, a town in Orange County starting to look very suburban. Quickly pedal out of the sprawl into the open countryside of Rt. 17M. You might wish to stop at Museum Village, an interesting re-creation of an old-time village, complete with blacksmith. Next, head through Sugar Loaf, a working crafts center that is becoming a popular tourist stop. The hill giving the village its name is spectacular to see in the fall.

Warwick has some beautiful large homes on its Main Street. Turning west, pass the quiet and charming Pacem in Teris ("Peace on Earth") meditation center, an outdoor sculpture garden by a stream run by author and philosopher Frederick Franck. Head toward Pine Island on pretty, rolling back roads with few cars. The small hamlet of Amity has some interesting old buildings and a pretty church.

Pine Island has a huge expanse of flat fields with rich, black soil, perfect for growing onions and other veggies. Ride by in late summer at harvest time and the aroma of onions is almost overpowering. The farmer's market has unbelievably low prices on local produce. A large pannier might be advisable to hold your purchases!

Ride north through more farms (and along Onion Ave., of course). Bypass Florida (Florida, N.Y., that is) and head for Chester. Uptown Chester has some interesting antique shops while historic downtown Chester looks like a Hollywood set—a set of very old storefronts awaiting restoration and a new life.

Cyclists doing the whole distance have a reward awaiting them in Washingtonville—a tour and tasting at Brotherhood Winery, which bills itself as the nation's oldest.

MONROE-PINE ISLAND (continued)

Directions to Starting Point: The route begins at the junction of **Routes 208 and 17M in Monroe.** Take the New York Thruway to Exit 16, then follow Rt. 17 West 4 miles to Exit 130. Turn left onto Rt. 208 South, and proceed under a mile to the junction of Rt. 17M. Parking is available in several nearby shopping centers and near the park with the lake.

POINT TO POINT	CUME	TURN	STREET/LANDMARK
0.0	0.0		From the intersection of Rt. 17M and Rt. 208, go **West** on **Rt. 17M**
			Museum Village will be on the right in about one mile
5.0	5.0	L	**County Rt. 13** toward Sugar Loaf and Warwick (first left after going over Rt. 17). After the turn, you will go under Rt. 17
2.5	7.5		Entering **Sugar Loaf** craft village
6.3	13.8	L	**Main St./Rt. 94** (T)
0.2	14.0	BL	At light to continue on **Rt. 94**
3.2	17.2	R	**Fancher Rd.** (by "Emmerich Greenhouse" sign)
0.4	17.6	R	**Covered Bridge Rd.** (T). **Pacem in Teris** Meditation Center on left after crossing the stream
0.0	17.6	L	**Onderdonk Rd.** (T)
1.7	19.3	R	**Blooms Corners Rd.** (T)
0.9	20.2	L	**Newport Rd.**
1.3	21.5	BR	At yield sign. Road name changes to **Newport Bridge Rd.**
0.1	21.6	L	To continue on **Newport Bridge Rd.** You are in the hamlet of Amity
1.5	23.1	R	At stop sign onto **Glenwood Rd.** (no street sign)
1.9	25.0	L	**Pine Island Turnpike/County Rt. 1** (toward Westtown)
0.2	25.2		Pine Island **Farmers Produce Market** on left
0.5	25.7	R	Toward Port Jervis to continue on **Pine Island Turnpike** (store on left after turn)
2.4	28.1	R	Toward **Middletown** onto **County Rt. 12** (no street sign)
4.7	32.8	R	**Onion Ave.** (next right after Pierce Circle)
0.7	33.5		Road becomes dirt
0.8	34.3		Pavement returns
0.5	34.8	R	**Maple Ave.** (T; no sign)

continued

MONROE-PINE ISLAND (continued)

POINT TO POINT	CUME	TURN	STREET/LANDMARK
1.6	36.4	R	**County Rt. 42** (toward Orange Farm)
1.2	37.6	L	**County Rt. 6** (toward Orange Farm and Goshen) (T)
0.7	38.3	R	**County Rt. 68** (toward Orange County Dept. of Social Services)
0.9	39.2	R	**Rt. 17A** (T)
0.6	39.8	L	**Durland Rd.**
0.7	40.5	L	**Rt. 94** (T)
3.3	43.8	R	At T to continue on **Rt. 94 North**
0.2	44.0	L	At traffic light to continue on **Rt. 94 North** Riders wishing to pedal the 49.5 miles, go **straight** here on **Rt. 17M**. Follow Rt. 17M 5.5 miles to the junction of Rt. 208 and the end of the route
0.2	44.2	L	At T in Chester business district to continue on **Rt. 94 North**
0.3	44.5	R	**Main St.** (sign for historic downtown Chester)
0.3	44.8	BR	**Railroad Ave.**
0.1	44.9	BR	**Greycourt Ave.**
0.0	44.9	L	**Meadow Ave.** Go under railroad immediately
1.4	46.3	R	**Rt. 94** (T)
0.9	47.2		Roe's **Orchards** on left
5.4	52.6	L	**North St.** (at Gulf station; past Rt. 208 intersection)
0.2	52.8	R	**Brotherhood Winery.** After touring winery, cycle back on **North St.** the way you came
0.2	53.0	R	**E. Main St.** (T)
0.1	53.1	L	**Rt. 208 South**
7.0	60.1	BR	To continue on **Rt. 208**
0.4	60.5		**Junction Rts. 17M and 208** (end of route)

MONROE-MONTGOMERY   48.9 miles

Terrain: A few hilly spots, but mostly just rolling.
Traffic: Very light to moderate near Montgomery and Walden and on Rt. 32. One mile of busy Rt. 17K.
Road Conditions: Good throughout. No dirt.
Points of Interest: Pleasant Orange County **farm and backwoods** scenery; **Museum Village** in Monroe; **Hill-Hold Farmstead Museum;** Nice quiet town of **Montgomery;** large dam at **Walden; Bethlehem Art Gallery** (many interesting Hudson Valley prints); Magnificent view of **Schunemunk Mt. railroad trestle;** Gasho Steakhouse **Japanese gardens.**

If quiet, rural back roads are your fancy, this is an ideal pedal. Head from the growing village of Monroe toward the still-quiet towns of Montgomery and Walden. In between, enjoy fields, woods, views, and serene cycling.

The first point of interest is near Montgomery. Orange County has a huge park here, which includes the Hill-Hold Farmstead Museum and a ski slope. It's worth a side trip to the top of the ski slope for the commanding view of the Wallkill Valley.

Montgomery has some charming small homes on Clinton and Bridge streets. Next head alongside the Wallkill River to Walden, an old industrial town with a large dam visible from the Main Street bridge.

Head south and east adjacent to Stewart Airport. The Bethlehem Art Gallery is worth a stop to see some beautiful prints of the Hudson Valley. They often have a picture of a view you will see a mile up the road—the large railroad trestle coming out of Schunemunk Mountain. Taylor Rd. heads practically right next to this mountain, a wilderness area owned by Star Expansion Co. and open to hikers.

On the final leg of the trip, you might wish to stop and see the formal Japanese gardens at Gasho Restaurant (please leave your bikes in the parking lot). Perhaps stop inside and make reservations for a later dinner—the chefs cook it right at your table.

Directions to Starting Point: The route begins at the junction of **Routes 208 and 17M in Monroe.** Take the New York Thruway to Exit 16, then follow Rt. 17 West 4 miles to Exit 130. Turn left onto Rt. 208 South, and proceed under a mile to the junction of Rt. 17M. Parking is available in several nearby shopping centers and near the park with the lake.

MONROE-MONTGOMERY (continued)

POINT TO POINT	CUME	TURN	STREET/LANDMARK
0.0	0.0		Starting at the intersection of Rts. 17M and 208, ride **North** on **Rt. 208**
0.3	0.3	L	To continue on **Rt. 208 North**
0.2	0.5	BL	Onto unmarked road with a **lake** on your right (Rt. 208 heads right and goes over Rt. 17)
0.8	1.3	R	At stop sign (no street sign) onto **Museum Village Rd.** (Go left here for **Museum Village**). Cross over Rt. 17
0.1	1.4	L	**Old Mansion Rd.**
1.0	2.4	R	**Oxford Rd.** (T)
1.1	3.5	S	Road changes name to **Craigsville Rd.** as Oxford Rd. bears right
1.4	4.9	L	**Rt. 94** (T)
0.1	5.0	R	**County Rt. 51**
0.2	5.2	BR	To continue on **County Rt. 51/Hulsetown Rd.**
2.1	7.3	L	At curve to continue on **County Rt. 51** (route sign is around the corner)
2.5	9.8	L	At stop sign onto **County Rt. 8**
0.0	9.8	R	Immediate **right** onto **County Rt. 77**
1.8	11.6	SR	**Rt. 207** (T)
0.4	12.0	L	**Rt. 416**
0.8	12.8		**Hill-Hold Farmstead Museum** on right
0.8	13.6		Turn **left** for county golf course and ski area with beautiful view
2.8	16.4	R	**Rt. 211 East** (T). **Bakery** on right after turn
1.3	17.7	L	**Clinton St.**
0.1	17.8	R	**Bridge St.** (T)
0.1	17.9	S	At stop sign onto **Rt. 17K.** Cross the bridge over the Wallkill River
0.1	18.0	R	After crossing the bridge onto **County Rt. 29**
3.6	21.6	R	**Cross St.**
0.1	21.7	R	**Main St.** (T)
0.3	22.0	R	At second light in Walden onto **Rt. 208 South**
0.5	22.5	L	**Coldenham Rd./County Rt. 75** (by Xtra gas station)
2.9	25.4	L	**Rt. 17K** (T)
1.2	26.6	R	**South Drury Lane**
3.5	30.1	L	**Rt. 207** (T)
0.4	30.5	R	**Station Rd.** and **Church Rd.** (double street sign)
0.0	30.5	L	**Kings Dr.** (T)

continued

MONROE-MONTGOMERY (continued)

POINT TO POINT	CUME	TURN	STREET/LANDMARK
0.7	31.2	R	**Rt. 207** (T)
0.4	31.6	R	**Lake Rd.** and **Jackson Ave.** (double street sign)
1.1	32.7	L	**Jackson Ave.**
1.8	34.5		**Bethlehem Art Gallery** on left
0.5	35.0	S	At stop sign. Cross Rt. 94
0.5	35.5	L	**Orrs Mills Rd.**
0.0	35.5	R	Immediate **right** to continue on **Jackson Ave.** Magnificent view of railroad trestle to your right
0.5	36.0	R	**Otter Kill Rd.** (T)
0.1	36.1	L	Quick **left** onto **Taylor Rd.**
1.6	37.7	R	**Angola Rd.** (T; yield sign; no street sign)
0.1	37.8	BR	**Rt. 32 South** (stop sign)
4.9	42.7		**Deli** on left in Highland Mills
0.8	43.5		**Gasho Restaurant** on right. Beautiful Japanese formal gardens behind restaurant
0.6	44.1	R	At blinking yellow light onto **Dunderberg Rd.**
0.0	44.1	L	To continue on **Dunderberg Rd.** (Edgewood Dr. goes right)
1.3	45.4	R	**Nininger Rd./County Rt. 64** (T)
1.4	46.8	L	At T (no street sign). Cross Rt. 17
0.6	47.4	BR	At fork onto **Spring St.**
0.7	48.1	L	Toward Business District. Go under railroad
0.1	48.2	R	At T, following signs for Business District
0.3	48.5	R	**Mill Pond Rd.** (traffic light)
0.4	48.9		**Junction Rts. 17M and 208** (end of route)

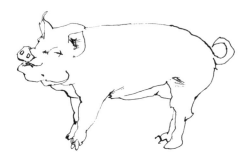

MONROE-MONTGOMERY
(48.9 miles)

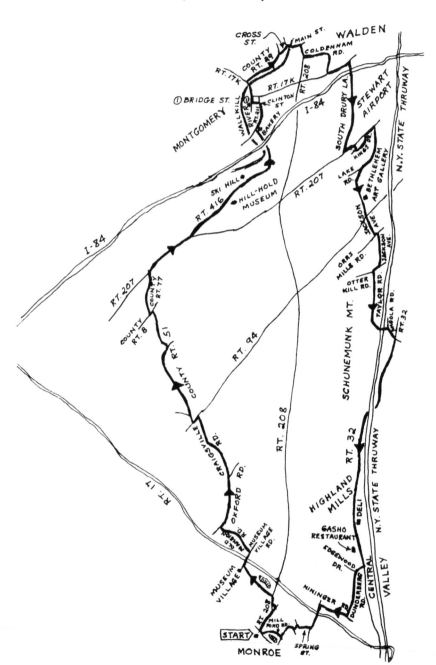

APPENDIX

TWO-WHEELED WEEKENDS

The following represents a very selective list of inns in the area covered by this guide. There are many other fine motels, campgrounds and other accommodations in the area.

HOMESTEAD INN
420 Field Pt. Rd.
Greenwich, CT 06830
(203) 869-7500

WEST LAKE INN
Ridgefield, CT 06877
(203) 438-7323

BEAR MOUNTAIN INN
Bear Mountain, NY 10911
(914) 786-2731

HUDSON HOUSE
2 Main St.
Cold Spring, NY 10516
(914) 265-9355